# THE FINAL WORLD EMPIRE

A 'REVIVED ROMAN EMPIRE' IN EUROPE

PAUL GARRATT

WESTBOW
PRESS
A DIVISION OF THOMAS NELSON
& ZONDERVAN

Copyright © 2014 Paul Garratt.

All rights reserved. No part of this book may be used or reproduced by any means, graphic, electronic, or mechanical, including photocopying, recording, taping or by any information storage retrieval system without the written permission of the publisher except in the case of brief quotations embodied in critical articles and reviews.

The copyright of the manuscript rests with the author and no quotation from it or information derived from it may be published without the prior consent of the author.

WestBow Press books may be ordered through booksellers or by contacting:

WestBow Press
A Division of Thomas Nelson & Zondervan
1663 Liberty Drive
Bloomington, IN 47403
www.westbowpress.com
1 (866) 928-1240

Because of the dynamic nature of the Internet, any web addresses or links contained in this book may have changed since publication and may no longer be valid. The views expressed in this work are solely those of the author and do not necessarily reflect the views of the publisher, and the publisher hereby disclaims any responsibility for them.

Any people depicted in stock imagery provided by Thinkstock are models, and such images are being used for illustrative purposes only. Certain stock imagery © Thinkstock.

Scripture quotations taken from the HOLY BIBLE, NEW INTERNATIONAL VERSION. Copyright © 1973, 1978, 1984 by International Bible Society. All rights reserved. "NIV" is a registered trademark of International Bible Society. UK trademark number 1448790.

ISBN: 978-1-4908-4081-9 (sc)
ISBN: 978-1-4908-4082-6 (e)

Library of Congress Control Number: 2014910809

Printed in the United States of America.

WestBow Press rev. date: 7/24/2014

CONTENTS

Dedication vii
Foreword by Dr. Ray Kirkland ix
Preface xi
Introduction xiii

Chapter 1   Background to the Book of Daniel 1
Chapter 2   A dazzling statue and four wild beasts 9
Chapter 3   A golden head and a winged lion 16
Chapter 4   A silver chest and a bear 22
Chapter 5   Bronze thighs and a four-headed leopard 29
Chapter 6   The Little Horns 33
Chapter 7   Iron mixed with clay and a terrifying beast 38
Chapter 8   The Son of Man and a heavenly kingdom 47
Chapter 9   The gap 52
Chapter 10 The fourth beast in the New Testament 57
Chapter 11 The Roman Catholic Church and the woman
            riding the beast 70
Chapter 12 The story so far 76
Chapter 13 Life beyond the grave! 77

Chapter 14   Charlemagne..83

Chapter 15   The Holy Roman Empire 92

Chapter 16   The Reformation 96

Chapter 17   The French Empire..103

Chapter 18   The German Empire 109

Chapter 19   The Third Reich..113

Chapter 20   The European Union 120

Chapter 21   Babylon in Europe 129

Chapter 22   What happens next? 133

Chapter 23   The conclusion of the matter................................136

Select Bibliography..143

DEDICATION

This book is dedicated to my wonderful brothers: Neil, Mark and Jamie. Your love of the Bible, passion for politics and fascination with history has inspired this work.

With special thanks to John Smith for the countless hours of proofreading that have helped to turn this work into a reality.

FOREWORD BY DR. RAY KIRKLAND

For nearly 40 years I have studied eschatology and accompanied it with extensive travel to 96 countries of the world. A common thread I see worldwide and through all of mankind is the desire to know how it all ends.

Paul Garratt's *The Final World Empire* draws a parallel of Old Testament writings and historical truths to end-time revelatory writings and contemporary, present-day occurrences. The book is a journey layered with births and wars, covenants and alliances, as he steps us through history using the wisdom of biblical paradigms.

The understanding of history as it is presented here is an invaluable resource. History has in fact aligned to the Word of God and continues to do so. It brings an assuring confidence that God's word is true, to the believer as well as to the critic.

This book belongs in the library of every serious bible student and historian.

Dr. Ray Kirkland
Executive Director for Church on the Rock International

PREFACE

Have you ever wondered if the current affairs of your nation are expressly spoken about in the Bible? I certainly have – especially as I witness my own country being entangled ever more bindingly in a web of bureaucracy spun by the European Union! Regardless of the political party elected to govern, Britain has somehow mysteriously moved into an ever-closer union with its continental neighbours at a staggering economic and political cost, for seemingly little reward. Furthermore, since the Eurozone crisis, in which ten European banks asked for a bailout during 2009, the question over the United Kingdom's future in relation to the EU has dominated the political arena in Westminster, and perhaps will prove to be the most topical issue at the next General Election in 2015.

It was both the mystery of this 'gravitational pull' towards Brussels, and the global impact caused by the Eurozone crisis, that prompted the question: does the Bible have anything to say about Europe, and if so, what? After three years of study, and to my own genuine surprise, I discovered that the Bible has a lot to say about Europe! Disturbingly, the current evolution of the European Union is intrinsically related to the ascendance of the final world empire – an empire ruled by the antichrist.

Starting in Babylon with a young Jewish captive named Daniel, this book explains God's detailed description of the rise and fall of four successive world empires until the permanent establishment of His kingdom on the earth. As we race from the courts of Babylon through the subsequent two and a half millennia of history, the precise fulfilment of the Danielic prophecies will become startlingly apparent. In particular, we will focus on the repeated process of death and resurrection found in the fourth empire and how each 'revival' has led to a significant new development in its character.

Many have sought to undertake the task of identifying the fourth empire or kingdom of the world, especially in its final form described by the apostle John in the Book of Revelation. Countless scholarly treatises have been written, and innumerable websites are dedicated to this task. Therefore it is difficult to claim that this book has somehow settled the debate and stands unique. However, on the basis of the work I have studied, three notable differences in this book are present. Twice in Revelation John was reminded that divine wisdom is needed to understand visions relating to the end of time. So although thorough academic research has been carried out, the primacy has been prayer in the Holy Spirit for wisdom and revelation. This in turn has led me to a literal understanding and interpretation of Bible prophecy above a figurative approach. And finally, this combination of intimacy with the Lord and a literal approach has produced a work that provides harmonious answers to the complex questions that beleaguer students in this area of study.

The most sensitive of such questions concerns the Roman Catholic Church. I trust that this book will encourage both Catholics and Protestants to understand our common origin and glorious future as the Bride of Christ. Just as Issachar was commended for understanding the signs of the times, this book will enable both Catholics and Protestants to anticipate that which will come next, and how together we might be an effective witness of Christ in this most exciting and exhilarating closing chapter of human history.

I pray that the heart of every reader might be touched by the loving presence and power of the Holy Spirit. Amen.

INTRODUCTION

Although the term 'revived Roman Empire' has become a popular phrase in certain charismatic circles – and certainly one that conjures all manner of vivid eschatological musings – a rather complex study must be conducted to use the term 'revival' and 'Roman Empire' in conjunction with one another. Rather than starting with the prophet Daniel's revelation of four successive world empires that would span the course of human history, we begin by considering the origin and significance of the city in which the revelations took place. It will become clear at the outset of our journey that Babylon, and its founder Nimrod, stand as a threefold type: the antichrist, his city and his religious system. As such, Babylon, the antithesis of Jerusalem, is a prophetic picture of what is yet to come. When we finally reach the climax of world history during the final stage of the fourth empire, it will become clear during our study of Revelation 17 and 18 both why and how the city of Babylon returns to the biblical spotlight.

Daniel's detailed description of the four successive world empires has led to many interesting conjectures being put forward over the years that attempt to identify them from history. Generally speaking, such conjectures fall into two schemes. The traditional conservative scheme presents the four empires or kingdoms as: Neo-Babylonian, Medo-Persian, Greek and Roman. The alternative scheme, which has gathered fresh support in recent years, separates the Medo-Persian Empire into two separate empires; this in turn results in a Grecian fourth empire. Although this view varies by one empire, for the modern day reader it has a profound implication on the relevance of Daniel's prophecies and their biblical counterparts. If it can be proved that the fourth empire was in fact Grecian, Daniel's description of divine judgement on this kingdom, and the subsequent arrival of God's own kingdom on earth, are relegated to the past – having already been fulfilled at the birth of Jesus Christ just after the death of the Greek Empire. Such a conclusion shuts the door on our attempt to understand the prophetic significance of the days in which we live.

However, it will become clear that the traditional view is the only viable interpretation on the count of history and Bible prophecy. Our survey of the two and a half millennia that make up the history of our world since the days of Daniel, can leave us in no doubt that the fourth empire was in fact the Roman Empire. Furthermore, the Roman Empire unerringly fulfils Daniel's description of the fourth world empire and exhibits numerous characteristics of ancient Babylonian religion and ideology. By taking a fresh new look at Gabriel's prophecy of the 'seventy weeks', we will discover that Daniel learned of a gap of an undetermined number of years between the death of Jesus Christ and a final three-and-a-half year period of time. During this time, the fourth empire would somehow endure over two thousand years and still be present in some form to this very day.

Our survey of history will prove beyond any doubt that although the Roman Empire had a birth and evolution comparable to many other empires from antiquity, its demise and death was altogether distinct, and therefore unique. Despite its official collapse in the West in 476, the empire continued in the East until 1453. It was during this time, and in the very location in which axe-wielding Germanic barbarians decisively defeated the Western Roman Empire, that a continuous and uninterrupted pattern of 'revival' and resurrection becomes apparent. We will not only compare and contrast each episode of 'revival' in European history with its counterpart from antiquity, but also with the picture we paint of the fourth world empire at the close of world history. This will enable us to trace the significant developments in each 'revival' and anticipate what is likely to happen next.

This journey through history will enable us to understand why Europe stands as the bloodiest continent on earth – a continent that no empire or ruler has successfully either tamed or united since the days of Charlemagne and the Frankish Empire. Following Charlemagne's death, the Frankish Empire fragmented and a three-way power struggle ensued between the emerging countries of France and Germany, and the pontiff in Rome. This ongoing power struggle over the centuries, culminating in the devastating World Wars of the last century, will be revealed as the result of a cosmic struggle for the establishment of the final world empire, and with it, the birth and ascendance of the antichrist.

During our study of the Second World War, we will unveil the motive and intention that lay behind the unparalleled manifestation of anti-Semitism in Nazi Germany. In doing so, the otherwise mysterious plight and suffering of the Jewish people since the death of Jesus Christ will be understood. Maintaining a focus on the Jewish people during each 'revival' will undoubtedly lead us to understand God's ultimate intention in bringing His chosen people back to the land of Israel after the Holocaust, to rebuild a temple and await the return of Jesus Christ after accepting him as the Messiah.

In the wake of Europe's failure as a continent, epitomised by the Second World War, two very distinct and highly significant events took place, almost simultaneously. The year 1948 saw Israel once again recognised as the nation state of the Jewish people. As a result, the city of Jerusalem, as Gabriel informed Daniel, and to the displeasure of liberal scholars who had long since replaced the city with the Church, returned to her rightful place as the centre stage of Bible prophecy. Less than a decade later, in a bid to repair a broken continent, the European Coal and Steel Community created an economic union that, in time, evolved into the European Union.

Just as Jerusalem was restored, so too through the EU the invisible workings of the spirit of Babylon in Europe became outwardly manifest. We will explore some of the staggering imagery adopted by the EU. Such imagery has provoked no small storm of conjecture and suspicion within countless Christian circles, and for good reason. The European Parliament building appears to have been based on a painting of the unfinished Tower of Babel; a woman riding a beast is the prolific icon of the EU; Berlin is now home to the Ishtar Gate and the Processional Way from Babylon – not to mention a recreated Pergamon Altar, the seat of Satan. As we consider the meaning of this Babylonian imagery, along with the prevailing humanist agenda, it will become clear that the EU marks a significant step towards the final world empire that will arise in the near future.

As we reach the end of our journey it will have become very clear that Bible prophecy has been precise and emphatic in revealing the chain of events that constitute our history. Therefore, on the sure foundation provided by God's written word, we spend time in John's Apocalypse gazing into the future to see what is likely to happen next. With great joy and eager anticipation the reader can enter tomorrow with a full assurance that God is truly in control. For these days, the ones in which you now live, are the glorious days in which the bride prepares to meet the bridegroom. The coming king is about to return. *Maranatha.*

CHAPTER 1

BACKGROUND TO THE BOOK OF DANIEL

It would be a mistake to start with King Nebuchadnezzar's visions of four kingdoms in Daniel 2, or even prior to that with the commencement of the ministry of Daniel in Babylon, without first considering the history and religion of the city that became his home. Although reading the twelve chapters of Daniel should leave us both amazed as to the accuracy of his prophecies and deeply convicted by the integrity of his lifestyle, an understanding of what Babylon was like elevates Daniel and his ministry to an even higher plane of excellence.

> *Cush was the father of Nimrod, who became a mighty warrior on the earth. ⁹ He was a mighty hunter before the Lord; that is why it is said, "Like Nimrod, a mighty hunter before the Lord." ¹⁰ The first centres of his kingdom were Babylon, Uruk, Akkad and Kalneh, in Shinar. ¹¹ From that land he went to Assyria, where he built Nineveh, Rehoboth Ir, Calah ¹² and Resen, which is between Nineveh and Calah—which is the great city. Genesis 10:8-12*

The city of Babylon makes an emphatic entrance to our Bibles in Genesis chapter 10 as the capital of the kingdom of Nimrod, son of Cush and great-grandson of Noah. A slight mistranslation may cause us to think that Nimrod was famous because of his hunting skills, which somehow impressed the Lord to such a degree that this detail found its way into the Bible! However, a more accurate translation of Genesis 10:9 would read: 'Like Nimrod, a mighty hunter in defiance of the Lord.' This description of Nimrod starts to make sense when we consider Nimrod's name, made up from the Hebrew word *marad*, meaning 'rebel.' Rather than a positive and godly character, in Nimrod we find quite the opposite, an individual who was rebellious against the Lord, and in his rebellion, built the city of Babylon.

At this point we need to ask two questions: why would Nimrod want to build a city in rebellion against the Lord, and for what purpose? There are two probable answers to this question: one is the ambition and intention of Satan; the other is the ambition and intention of Nimrod. The spirit of antichrist was at work in the Garden of Eden when the serpent told Eve that she would become like God if she would eat the fruit from the tree of the knowledge of good and evil. Here, the maddening irony of Satan's mission becomes apparent. Having lost his own position in heaven for seeking to rival God, Satan then sows the same insatiable desire into man – that he should seek to become equal to his creator by throwing off the limitations that God had placed upon him. The spirit of antichrist can be seen working in this regard throughout Bible history, especially that of Israel, which climaxed at the crucifixion of Christ when his own countrymen, only days after welcoming him with olive branches, rejected him in favour of Barabbas – a man who sought to achieve justice by his own hands. Babylon and Nimrod were therefore the literal manifestation of antichrist. In Babylon, man thought he was the master of his own destiny, just as their leader Nimrod proclaimed to be, and yet, in this deception, Satan was the one behind the scenes who was receiving the glory and worship of man.

Whether Nimrod understood the power and influence of the spirit of antichrist remains to be seen. However, the Jewish historian Josephus, writing in the first century, shared the then commonly held view about Nimrod that answers both questions:

> *Now it was Nimrod who excited them to such an affront and contempt of God. He was the grandson of Ham, the son of Noah-a bold man, and of great strength of hand.*

He persuaded them not to ascribe it to God, as if it were through his means they were happy, but to believe that it was their own courage which procured that happiness. He also gradually changed the government into tyranny-seeing no other way of turning men from the fear of God, but to bring them into a constant dependence upon his own power.

He also said he would be revenged on God, if he should have a mind to drown the world again; for that he would build a tower too high for the waters to be able to reach! and that he would avenge himself on God for destroying their forefathers! (Antiquities. I: iv: 2)

If Josephus was correct, Nimrod had founded this post-flood kingdom on a religion in which the people were to depend on their own courage and efforts to produce security and happiness, rather than God. Nimrod used his own might and courage in hunting wild animals to set an example of how to live. The overriding reason for this was anger at God for sending the flood and destroying the previous way of life on the earth, which we know from the account of Noah was one of absolute depravity and rebellion.

The view of Josephus is not without supporting evidence. In the ancient literature of the Sumerians, Babylonians, Assyrians and Hittites, a character called Gilgamesh is described, who is very similar to Josephus' description of Nimrod. As with numerous other extra-biblical works, the story of Gilgamesh combines certain facts with myths and legends that were peculiar to those recounting the story. The collected artefacts relating to Gilgamesh are now known as 'The Gilgamesh Epic.' There are numerous translations of the epic, all of which portray Gilgamesh, or Nimrod, as a depraved ruler of people, who raped women, ferociously hunted wild animals and sought to oppose God because of the flood that destroyed the former civilizations of earth.

It now becomes clear why Nimrod built the tower of Babel. It was not a tower or ziggurat that was simply taller than others that had been built; rather it was a symbol of man's independence from God and defiance of Him; for if God should flood the earth again, the tower would remain as a symbol of man's independence from Him. The peak of the tower was meant to penetrate the heavens, declaring war on God for relegating man to the earth. This spirit of rebellion and defiance against God, that was set in the foundation of Babylon, would remain over the coming centuries and attract other forms of wickedness and evil.

This is precisely what happened. Extra-biblical sources inform us that it was highly likely that Shem executed Nimrod for his crime of apostasy. Semiramis, Nimrod's wife, continued to perpetuate the tyranny her husband had begun. Eventually Nimrod was deified and worshipped as a Messiah, whose death was voluntary, for his blood was believed to take away the curse on the world allowing a new creation to begin. It was taught that Nimrod came back to life as a son of Semiramis. This in turn elevated Semiramis, who was celebrated as the virgin mother of Nimrod, the son of the God.

The Tower of Babel. Engraved by Isaac Basire and published in The Works of Flavius Josephus.

This certainly is consistent if we consider the archaeological discoveries of the last century that provide a startling insight into the language, culture and religion of the Sumerians, the descendents and followers of Semiramis who dwelt in Babylon. The Sumerians were monotheistic, worshipping 'An' the Skygod. Over time, 'Innini' was introduced as the Earth-goddess, acting as a consort to the Skygod. The fifth antediluvian king, Dumuzi, was given the title 'son of the gods.' He was believed to have been the son of Innini, who willingly sacrificed himself for his mother. The story then developed into a legend in which Innini descends to the abode of the dead to seek out Dumuzi whilst leaving the earth barren and longing for her return.

When the Akkadians, of Semitic descent, settled in Babylon after the time of the Sumerians, they uncovered a seemingly more advanced religion than their own. Indeed, it was as if the spirit of Babylon was already so powerful that it captivated the hearts and minds of the Akkadians to such a degree that they adopted much of this new religion. Innini was renamed 'Ishtar', the planet Venus, whom the Akkadians also called the Queen of heaven. 'Tammuz,' the son of Ishtar, played the role of Dumuzi, who died on behalf of his mother. The interesting feature added to this evolving religion was the resurrection of Tammuz from the dead. This fusion of religion produced the very foundation upon which every form of paganism would be built: a dying son of an earth-goddess. A virgin mother and her son were worshipped in Egypt, Greece, Turkey, Rome, China, Tibet and Japan.

After the days of Nimrod, the history of Babylon from both biblical and extra-biblical sources becomes quite vague, partly because for the succeeding millennia and a half, Babylon itself was relegated from the centre stage of world politics to that of a small pawn of Assyrian politics. However, in 626 BC the Chaldean general Nabopolassar defected from his Assyrian employers and crowned himself king of the Babylonians. Not only did this act of defiance put the city of Babylon back onto the world stage, it also marked the beginning of what we now call the 'Neo-Babylonian' dynasty.

After successful alliances with the Medes and Scythians, which involved his eight-year-old son Nebuchadnezzar II[1] marrying the Median princess Amuhean, Nabopolassar laid a three-month siege on the Assyrian powerbase of Nineveh. Eventually, the gates of the city opened in submission to the invaders, but mercy was not shown; the city was completely obliterated and its inhabitants either massacred or sold into slavery. The ferocity and violence that poured into Nineveh communicated two messages to the Near East. First, it demonstrated revenge for ruthless treatment of Babylon during the past two thousand years of occupation, and second, it was an opportunity for Nabopolassar to demonstrate that a new kingdom from the ancient city of Babylon had been born.

---

1   Hereafter we will refer to Nebuchadnezzar II as Nebuchadnezzar.

This decisive moment in ancient history saw the Assyrians retreat to Carchemish and make allegiance with the Egyptian army of Pharaoh Necco II. Nebuchadnezzar, son of Nabopolassar, marched against Carchemish in 605 BC. Necco II came to aid the Assyrian king Ashuruballit II, but was met by resistance at Megiddo by King Josiah of Judah. Such resistance was futile; the armies of Judah were comprehensively defeated and the corpse of Josiah was returned to Jerusalem to be buried near the tomb of King David. Although victorious at Megiddo, both the Egyptians and the Assyrians were defeated at Carchemish in a battle of such magnitude, that the two thousand year old Assyrian Empire was brought to an abrupt end and the Egyptian Empire fell into a comatose state from which it would never recover.

Whilst visiting the British History Museum, I read the following extract from the Babylonian Chronicles that summarises the decisive victory of Nebuchadnezzar:

> "[Nebuchadnezzar] crossed the river to go against the Egyptian army which lay in Carchemish. The armies fought with each other and the Egyptian army withdrew before him. He accomplished their defeat and beat them to nonexistence. As for the rest of the Egyptian army which had escaped from the defeat so quickly that no weapon had reached them, the Babylonians overtook and defeated them in the district of Hamath so that not a single man escaped to his own country. At that time Nebuchadnezzar conquered the whole of Hatti-land."
> (The Jerusalem Chronicle ABC 5)

Now Babylon once again had risen from the backwaters as the ruling power in Mesopotamia, and so Judah, the southern part of Israel, had to submit to Babylonian rule.

Whilst Nebuchadnezzar was returning from this historic victory, he was met by a runner with the news that his father Nabopolassar had died. Although he was clearly the next in line to the throne, Nebuchadnezzar raced across the desert with a small bodyguard to seize the crown in Babylon. In less than a month Nebuchadnezzar had made the one thousand mile trip, arriving in Babylon on 7 September 605 BC, where he was crowned the new king of the Neo-Babylonian dynasty.

Nebuchadnezzar started his reign by rebuilding the Tower of Babel, erecting a ziggurat called the Etemenanki built over the site on which the old tower was thought to stand. In his own words Nebuchadnezzar records how he saw its rebuilding as a divine commission from the god Merodach (Marduk):

> *The tower, the eternal house, which I founded and built. I have completed its magnificence with silver, gold, other metals, stone, enamelled bricks, fir and pine. The first which is the house of the earth's base, the most ancient monument of Babylon; I built and finished it. I have highly exalted its head with bricks covered with copper. We say for the other, that is, this edifice, the house of the seven lights of the earth the most ancient monument of Borsippa. A former king built it, (they reckon 42 ages) but he did not complete its head. Since a remote time, people had abandoned it, without order expressing their words. Since that time the earthquake and the thunder had dispersed the sun-dried clay. The bricks of the casing had been split, and the earth of the interior had been scattered in heaps. Merodach, the great god, excited my mind to repair this building. I did not change the site nor did I take away the foundation. In a fortunate month, in an auspicious day, I undertook to build porticoes around the crude brick masses, and the casing of burnt bricks. I adapted the circuits, I put the inscription of my name in the Kitir of the portico. I set my hand to finish it. And to exalt its head. As it had been done in ancient days, so I exalted its summit.*[1]

During the reign of the Assyrians, Marduk had assumed the role of Tamuz, and was regarded as the son of Ishtar. Babylon hosted an annual mystery play, a sort of elaborate drama in which Marduk would die on behalf of his mother Ishtar, who in turn would leave the earth to look for him and raise him from the dead. This performance was acted out each year to coincide with the cycle of the sun. In 575 BC, the king had the Ishtar Gate built in dedication to her. The gate was decorated with three hundred and thirty-seven snake gods. In Hebrew numerology, three hundred and thirty-seven is the number of hell, and this gate was meant to symbolise the gateway to the underworld, literally the doorway to hell. The gate was the start of the processional way that led to the temple of Ishtar. Nebuchadnezzar was clearly indicating that Babylon was not only revived according to its ancient religious system, it was now the gateway to the spiritual underworld. It was at this city that Daniel arrived as a young man to start his transformational ministry!

The Ishtar Gate in the Pergamon Museum, Berlin

---

[1] John McClintock, James Strong, *Cyclopaedia of Biblical, Theological, and Ecclesiastical Literature,* New York: Harper & Brothers 1894 pp.465–469.

CHAPTER 2

A DAZZLING STATUE AND FOUR WILD BEASTS

Following his coronation in 605 BC, Nebuchadnezzar could no longer only concern himself with the stratagems of war and the building of pagan sites; he had to master the arts of diplomacy and political manoeuvrings. There was perhaps no other nation in his empire that helped him develop these skills more than Judah.

Despite two sieges in 605 and 597 BC, and the assured loyalty of two vassal kings, Jehoiakim and Jehoiachin, Zedekiah ignored the prophetic warnings of Jeremiah and became the last king of Judah. Nebuchadnezzar destroyed Jerusalem and led the remaining members of Judah into captivity.

During the first exodus Daniel was selected to serve in the Babylonian court as predicted in Isaiah 39:7 and 2 Kings 20:19. The prophetic utterances of Jeremiah and Isaiah had seen fulfilment; the temple in Jerusalem was ruined, the walls of the city had been torn down and Judah was now the captive of Babylon. For the Jews, their history and future was now a tale of two cities: the city of Babylon with the Etemenanki and gateway to hell, and the city of Jerusalem, home of the temple and throne of David. It was in this context of prophetic fulfilment that Daniel began to record his experiences:

> *[1] In the third year of the reign of Jehoiakim king of Judah, Nebuchadnezzar king of Babylon came to Jerusalem and*

> *besieged it. ² And the Lord delivered Jehoiakim king of Judah into his hand, along with some of the articles from the temple of God. These he carried off to the temple of his god in Babylonia and put in the treasure-house of his god. (Daniel 1:1-2)*

The significance of the time that Daniel's pen etched these first few words cannot be overlooked. Until this point, God had not revealed in a coordinated way, the future for His people beyond this current judgement. For the Jewish mind it was a question of what would happen next. So far, the prophecies concerning their exile and judgment had been painfully accurate, but those left unfulfilled about a forthcoming Messiah and Redeemer were lacking a context to which God's people could relate their current experiences or future hopes.

In order to emphasise the fact that he was writing to give a future hope to his own people and an outline of the future world history of the gentile nations, Daniel used a common type of literary device in his book to communicate and reinforce this message. Often readers are puzzled why Daniel did not write in chronological order. But this becomes clear when we consider the literary structure. In chapter 2 and verse 4, Daniel switched from writing in Hebrew, the language of the Jews, to Aramaic, the written language of the Babylonians. He continued to write in Aramaic until chapter 8 when he reverted back to Hebrew until the close of the book.

When we read the Book of Daniel according to this pattern, his ordering of events makes sense. Daniel starts in chapter 1 by explaining the fate of his own people at the hands of Nebuchadnezzar and his own rise to prominence. Chapters 2-7 start with the overview of gentile world history from the viewpoint of Nebuchadnezzar, followed by the fall of the Neo-Babylonians and the rise of the Medo-Persians. This section then closes with Daniel receiving a series of night visions that provide the same overview of gentile world history that Nebuchadnezzar saw in his dream. From chapter 8 to the close of the book, Daniel receives revelation about the future hope of the Jewish people to the coming of Jesus Christ and after his death to the end of the ages. This expels the myth that there were a number of silent years between the close of the

Old Testament and the start of the New Testament. A detailed picture of the future of the Jewish people is painted in the final Hebrew section of Daniel.

It is highly likely that Daniel had some divine insight from heaven that he was now living in the new season, labelled by Christ as 'the times of the Gentiles' (Luke 21:14). Therefore his selection to serve in Babylon was part of God's plan to bring light and clarity to his fellow countrymen before he started the written account. This would explain the agility with which Daniel was able to manoeuvre through the political maze of the Babylonian court. For certainly a God-fearing Hebrew who did not understand the significance of Nebuchadnezzar in God's redemptive plan would have refused to serve in his court, or resisted to the point of death his Jewish name being changed to the pagan one of Belteshazzar, the prince of Marduk – the god who ordered Nebuchadnezzar to rebuild the Etemenanki!

However Daniel did not use any heavenly insight as a license for sin and self-promotion. Far from it; when it came to the moral juncture of whether to eat the royal food, which almost certainly would have been sacrificed to idols, Daniel and his three friends were willing to risk their lives to honour the command of God to worship none other than Him. After eating vegetables for ten days, two remarkable promotions took place for Daniel, and his friends Hananiah, Mishael and Azariah. First, God blessed such dedication with an increase to their knowledge and understanding, with Daniel receiving an additional ability to interpret dreams and visions. Second, when the four friends from Judah had an audience with Nebuchadnezzar, they proved ten times wiser than any other wise men of his kingdom. As a result, they were invited into the king's personal advisory body.

In the second year of Nebuchadnezzar's reign, the wise men of Babylon were called into service to both explain and interpret a dream that had deeply disturbed the king. Interestingly, despite their promotion, Daniel, Hananiah, Mishael and Azariah were not present when Nebuchadnezzar first made his request:

> "This is what I have firmly decided: If you do not tell me the dream and interpret it, I will have you cut into pieces

> *and your houses turned into piles of rubble. But if you tell me the dream and explain it, you will receive from me gifts and rewards and great honour. So tell me the dream and interpret it for me." (Daniel 2:5-6)*

Many reasons have been set forth to explain why Nebuchadnezzar added the death penalty for failure to retell the dream and interpret it, the most common being that he himself had forgotten the dream. However, it is unlikely that an event that troubled the king to such a degree that he summoned his council of wise men immediately was somehow vague in his mind. It is far more likely that Nebuchadnezzar used the dream to test the ability of the large administration he had inherited from his father. Failure would have provided the king with the perfect opportunity to cut the wage bill and streamline the government. After the pleas of the enchanters and astrologers for more information about the dream was rejected, the official decree to begin the pogrom of all the wise men of Babylon was issued.

When this news reached Daniel, he went to the king and asked for time so that he might both tell Nebuchadnezzar his dream and interpret it. One can only imagine what a prayer meeting must have taken place with Daniel and his three friends that night. The boldness of Daniel was rewarded, for during the night, in a vision, the dream and its interpretation were given to him. Daniel immediately sought an audience with the king and, after giving the glory to God for the insight he had received, he described the dream.

Nebuchadnezzar had seen a giant dazzling statue composed of five materials: a head of gold, chest and arms of silver, belly and thighs of bronze, legs of iron, and feet of iron and partly baked clay. Whilst he watched the colossus, a rock was carved out by extraterrestrial hands and struck the statue on its feet, causing it to fall to the ground and smash into such small pieces that they were blown away by the wind. The stone then became a mountain that filled the whole earth.

Daniel then revealed to Nebuchadnezzar that the statue was composed of five different materials to symbolise four successive but doomed kingdoms. Daniel attributes the ultimate destruction of these kingdoms to the stone that struck the statue on its feet. The prophet explains that this stone is a kingdom that God will set up to endure forever. Upon hearing this, Nebuchadnezzar, the king of a pagan nation, the very genesis of which was in rebellion against God, fell at Daniel's feet and paid homage to the Lord.

The statue in Nebuchadnezzar's dream was designed to show four world kingdoms that are ultimately replaced by God's kingdom at the close of the age. The heathen king was able to view God's future plan of world history in its humanity: one figure, interconnected with a spectacular and almost heroic appearance. However, when it came to God's kingdom, Nebuchadnezzar was only able to understand it as a mere stone from a mountain.

This interpretation is the start of the biblical premise needed to examine the European Union. The final world kingdom must be one that endures or is in place when God's kingdom literally comes from heaven and overpowers all other world powers and fastens itself to earth. If this represents the Roman Empire, which has long since ceased, a future allegorical 'Roman Empire' can be expected.

Thankfully, over half a century later under the reign of Belshazzar, the last king of the Neo-Babylonian Kingdom, Daniel recorded his own series of visions concerning the four world kingdoms. The visions shed additional light on the meaning of the imposing statue that Nebuchadnezzar saw. Daniel closed the Aramaic section of his book in chapter 7 with this account:

> *In the first year of Belshazzar king of Babylon, Daniel had a dream, and visions passed through his mind as he was lying in bed. He wrote down the substance of his dream.*
> (Daniel 7:1)

Rather than the impressive statue, Daniel saw the world kingdoms from a heavenly perspective as four wild and aggressive beasts in conflict and turmoil. This was the inner and sub-human aspect of the kingdoms that would come on the earth. The first was like a lion, with the wings of an eagle, which had its wings torn off and was then made to stand on two feet like a man. The second was like a bear, which was commanded to eat its fill of flesh. The third was like a leopard with four wings on its back and four heads, and was given the authority to rule. The final beast was not compared to another animal, but had iron teeth and trampled its victims underfoot. This final beast had ten horns, three of which were uprooted by a small horn that had 'the eyes of a man and spoke boastfully.'[2] The final beast waged war on the saints and was victorious.

The visions came to a climax in a courtroom scene in which the Ancient of Days took His seat and books were opened. The fourth beast was slain and destroyed in a fire, whilst the other beasts were stripped of their power. Daniel then introduced the Son of Man, a mysteriously beautiful character who is led into God's presence and entrusted with an eternal kingdom and the guarantee of universal worship.

Daniel's vision of the four beasts

As with Nebuchadnezzar's dream, Daniel is instructed that the four beasts represent four kingdoms which will rise out of the earth, symbolised by the great sea as in Isaiah 51:10 and Revelation 17:8-24. The saints of the Most High are then given a kingdom for their eternal possession.

Here we find three clear reasons as to why the visions of Daniel are concerned with the same subject matter as the dream of Nebuchadnezzar over fifty years previously. First we have four kingdoms that succeed each other. Second, the first beast is the most noble of all animals, a lion, but as with the kingdoms, the animals decline until the advent of the fourth beast, which cannot be compared to any one animal. Third, the visions conclude with God's judgement on His enemies and the setting up of an eternal kingdom. This is the stone that destroys the statue and becomes an everlasting kingdom that fills the earth.

Although a clear interpretation of the visions was given to Daniel, he made further enquiries about the terrifying fourth beast. Daniel was then informed that this beast would be different from the other beasts and would have a universal reign. The ten horns represented ten kings who would come from this kingdom, prior to a final king coming who would be responsible for the persecution of Daniel's people. However, the court would judge in favour of the saints and the final king would be destroyed. The saints then receive an eternal kingdom and see the inhabitants of the earth worship God.

Given this understanding of the dream of Nebuchadnezzar and the visions of Daniel, that there would be four world kingdoms or empires, we can look back over the last two thousand five hundred years to identify these four kingdoms. Once the identity of the fourth kingdom is unveiled, we know with certainty that it will be present in some form when Jesus Christ returns with his heavenly kingdom.

---

[2]   Daniel 7:8.

CHAPTER 3

A GOLDEN HEAD AND A WINGED LION

A winged lion on the Ishtar Gate

To leave Nebuchadnezzar and his readers in no doubt over the identity of the first kingdom, Daniel states:

You, O king, are the king of kings. The God of heaven has given you dominion and power and might and glory; in your hands he has placed mankind and the beasts of the field and the birds of the air. Wherever they live, he has

made you ruler over them all. You are that head of gold.
(Daniel 2:37-38)

By providing us with the identity of the first kingdom, we can now turn our attention to the reasons for which God used a golden head to portray this first kingdom to Nebuchadnezzar, and a winged lion-like beast to Daniel. Whether these pictures communicate outward characteristics of the kingdom, the inner nature and workings of the kingdom, or entirely different aspects of Nebuchadnezzar's reign, the following three kingdoms should share the same likeness to their metaphors.

The Greek historian Herodotus visited Babylon just ninety years after the death of Nebuchadnezzar in 562 BC. Arguably, it was the vast amounts of gold he saw adorning the pagan sites of Babylon that left him with an indelible impression. Herodotus writes in detail about his astonishment at the quantity of gold used in the precincts of Bel, the Akkadian deity of Babylon. In the smaller temple of Marduk, Herodotus saw a table made of pure gold, whilst below in the second temple he saw the god made of gold seated on a golden throne with a golden base in front of a large golden table. Herodotus finished his account by describing an altar made of solid gold outside of the temple.

When we take Herodotus' account and consider alongside it the golden statue described by Daniel measuring ninety feet high and nine feet wide, which was built at Nebuchadnezzar's request, it becomes clear that this kingdom could justifiably be called the 'golden kingdom'.[3]

It becomes clear why Nebuchadnezzar used such a lavish amount of gold around the shrines and temples in Babylon when we consider his religious convictions. The East India House Inscription, currently in the British Museum London, records the desire of Nebuchadnezzar to bring gold and other costly items to the temple houses of his god Marduk:

> *Silver, gold, glitter or precious stones, copper, palm – wood, cedar, whatsoever thing is precious, in large abundance; the produce of mountains, the fullness of seas, a rich*

> *present, a splendid gift, to my city Babylon into his presence I brought.*[4]

The inscription also details Nebuchadnezzar decorating the walls of the temple of Marduk with costly stones, and overlaying the ceiling with gold.

Clearly God used gold as a literal description of the Neo-Babylonian Kingdom, but what of the head into which it was fashioned? Whereas the other metallic aspects of the statue Nebuchadnezzar saw in his dream consisted of multiple parts, the head was a single unit. This again was a very literal description to Nebuchadnezzar about the future of his kingdom. Each successive king would be supreme until the kingdom would come to an abrupt end. It would not fragment into multiple fiefdoms or share power with another.

Daniel himself chronicled the rise and fall of the Neo-Babylonian Empire as one that existed as a single unit. Interestingly, it was over an issue of gold that resulted in Belshazzar's ignominious death and the end of the Neo-Babylonian Empire. During a licentious gathering of the nobility, he called for the gold and silver goblets that were originally plundered from the temple in Jerusalem to be used by his guests. God ended the party with a message on the wall detailing Belshazzar's fate, and that very night the king was killed by Medo-Persians who took over the city.

In chapter 7 this first king or kingdom is described as a winged lion, which matches other biblical metaphors used by the prophets to describe Nebuchadnezzar as both a lion and an eagle.[5] Indeed, winged lions were a symbol of the Neo-Babylonian kings. A winged lion, excavated from Nimrud near Babylon, marks the entrance to the Babylonian section of the British Museum.

In the vision, the beast had its wings torn off and was made to stand on two feet like a man, whilst the heart of a man was given to it. The tearing off of wings, and gaining human like qualities is a reference to a rather bizarre set of events that occurred later in Nebuchadnezzar's reign. After receiving a troubling dream about a tree, the king summoned Daniel to provide the interpretation. It transpired that God was warning Nebuchadnezzar to turn from sin or risk becoming like an animal roaming the countryside away from the kingdom. This is exactly what happened; Nebuchadnezzar became insane and was driven from his people and lived in fields. However, when he looked up to heaven to acknowledge the Lord, his sanity was restored and he returned to the throne.

Although the story in itself serves to encourage us that God is always in control, the remarkable fact is that it was written by Nebuchadnezzar's own hand, making Daniel 4 a chapter written by the king of the most pagan nation on earth who had come to faith in the God of Daniel. Furthermore, the testimony of God's grace in the event was written in a letter and published throughout the Neo-Babylonian Kingdom. In Daniel 4 beginning at verse 34 we have this amazing testimony of the king:

> *At the end of that time, I, Nebuchadnezzar, raised my eyes toward heaven, and my sanity was restored. Then I praised the Most High; I honoured and glorified him who lives forever. His dominion is an eternal dominion; his kingdom endures from generation to generation. [35] All the peoples of the earth are regarded as nothing. He does as he pleases with the powers of heaven and the peoples of the earth. No one can hold back his hand or say to him: "What have you done?" [36] At the same time that my sanity was restored, my honour and splendour were returned to me for the glory of my kingdom. My advisers and nobles sought me out, and I was restored to my throne and became even greater than before. [37] Now I, Nebuchadnezzar, praise and exalt and glorify the King of heaven, because everything he does is right and all his ways are just. And those who walk in pride he is able to humble. (Daniel 4:34-37)*

We know from the interpretation that Daniel gave Nebuchadnezzar of his dream of the statue, that God had given the king universal dominion and power over all mankind, the birds of the air and the beasts of the field (Daniel 2:38). By referring to animals, God was emphasising that Nebuchadnezzar's rule was as absolute as possible. A similar and more explicit usage is found in Jeremiah 27:6: 'Now I will hand all your countries over to my servant Nebuchadnezzar king of Babylon; I will make even the wild animals subject to him.' This description of the supreme power Nebuchadnezzar had is demonstrated in the first beast in Daniel 7. Here, the beast is like a lion, the first among beasts, with the wings of an eagle, often known as a Griffon Vulture, first among the birds in the mysticism of the Eastern world.

However, there are two very obvious problems with this interpretation of the reign of Nebuchadnezzar and his successors. First, this empire did not hold sway over the entire earth, but rather that of the inhabited Asian world. Second, although it was the leading empire after the demise of the Assyrians, the Babylonians lived in some degree of fear of the growing Median kingdom. To protect Babylon from Median invasion Nebuchadnezzar built the Median Wall from Sippara on the Euphrates to the modern village of Jibra on the Tigris. This climate of fear towards Median attack certainly did not disappear as the Neo-Babylonian Empire developed. Nabonidus, the last king of Babylon, rejoiced at the news of the Persian triumph over the Medes at the hands of King Cyrus, perhaps hoping his own empire would now be safe.

Such historical evidence would seem to suggest that the vision of a lion with eagle's wings was a description of the political rather than military power possessed by Nebuchadnezzar and his successors. Throughout Daniel's record, there is never a disclosure of a Babylonian king being subject to any other law or power other than to God Himself. In chapter 2, Nebuchadnezzar ordered the execution of the entire advisory service his father had put in place for failure to reveal and interpret his dream. In chapter 3 he had a golden statue erected on the plains of Dura and commanded the execution of Daniel's companions Shadrach, Meshach and Abednego for failure to comply with the edict to bow before it.[6]

As we turn to the second kingdom, two important observations can be made. First, the gold used in the description of the Neo-Babylonian Empire speaks of the strength of its political leadership and ambition to rule, rather than the strength and force of its military. Second, the geography applied to the first kingdom was relative to the world to which it was acquainted, rather than the world as we have it today. There should be continuity of meaning when we consider similar phrases in the next aspects of the statue of chapter 2 and the beasts of chapter 7.

---

3   Daniel 3:1-2.
4   A. Sayce, Ed., "India House Inscription of Nebuchadnezzar, col. ii. 30-39", *Records of the Past, 2nd series,* 1890, < http://www.sacred-texts.com/ane/rp/rp203/rp20326.htm> [accessed 10 Oct 2010].
5   Jeremiah 4:7; 49:19; 50:17, 44; 49:22; Lamentations 4:19; Habakkuk 1:8; Ezekiel 17:3, 12.
6   Daniel 3:13-23.

CHAPTER 4

A SILVER CHEST AND A BEAR

On a winter's evening in 539 BC, whilst Belshazzar had the fateful encounter with the hand of God etching his own demise on the wall of his palace, Cyrus the Great and his troops finished diverting the river Euphrates away from Babylon. The water level of the river dropped to the depth of half a metre, enabling the Medo-Persian invaders to wade along the river and pass under the walls of the city. Because there was no great battle, it took several days for all the inhabitants of the city to realise that Babylon had been taken over, and even longer to understand that this marked the end of the Neo-Babylonian Empire.

Belshazzar's feast and the writing on the wall

However, once again, Daniel was already prepared for this change in power and manoeuvred himself into a position to honour the Lord before the new king of Babylon. Josephus records how Daniel greeted Cyrus when he officially entered Babylon with the scroll of Isaiah 44-45, written some hundred years before Cyrus was born, referring to Cyrus by name as the one who would help restore the fortunes of Jerusalem. Cyrus, duly impressed by the God of Daniel, sought to fulfil the prophecies made concerning his relationship with Judah:

> ²² *In the first year of Cyrus king of Persia, in order to fulfil the word of the Lord spoken by Jeremiah, the Lord moved the heart of Cyrus king of Persia to make a proclamation throughout his realm and also to put it in writing:* ²³ *"This is what Cyrus king of Persia says: "'The Lord, the God of heaven, has given me all the kingdoms of the earth and he has appointed me to build a temple for him at Jerusalem in Judah. Any of his people among you may go up, and may the Lord their God be with them.'" (2 Chronicles 36:22-23)*

In the British Museum, London, the Stele of Cyrus is displayed, which refers to Cyrus' non-biblical account of these events:

> *Without any battle, he entered the town, sparing any calamity;... I returned to sacred cities on the other side of the Tigris, the sanctuaries of which have been in ruins for a long time... and established for them permanent sanctuaries. I also gathered all their former inhabitants and returned them to their habitations.*[7]

However, it was not only the accuracy of the prophecy of Isaiah handed to the king that impressed him, but also the religion of the Babylonians. Although he was a Zoroastrian, Cyrus saw his triumph over Babylon as the will of Marduk whom Nebuchadnezzar had served so devoutly. As with the Akkadians centuries before him, another great religious fusion was about to take place in Babylon. The offspring of such a union was the cult of Mithras in its earliest form. Later, the Mithraic mysteries became a significant cult in the Roman Republic.

Before we examine the silver chest and arms of Nebuchadnezzar's statue and the bear like beast in Daniel's night visions, it is helpful to realise that we are about to enter one of the main battlegrounds presided over by conservative and liberal Bible scholars. The identity of this second kingdom is the key that unlocks the identity of the fourth kingdom. If the second kingdom is Medo-Persian, and we follow the sequence of history, the then known world is in turn dominated by the Greeks and then the Romans. This provides an opportunity to examine the possibility that the Roman Empire was never actually succeeded by another empire and may one day be, or already has been, revived. If however, it transpires that the second kingdom was Median, followed by the Persian Empire, the fourth kingdom becomes Greek. A Greek fourth empire or kingdom would mean that the prophetic elements at the end of the dream and visions in Daniel 2 and 7, have already been fulfilled and do not require us to assess the EU or any other post-Greek empire.

The Canon of Kings, sometimes known as the Canon of Ptolemy, supports the view that the second kingdom was Medo-Persian, the third Greek and the fourth Roman. The canon, created by astronomers in Babylon, was a chronology based on the reigns of kings that were seen as rulers over the known world, to which important astronomical events were linked. Its alternative name came from the famous Greek astronomer and mathematician Claudius Ptolemy, who worked on the canon during the ascendancy of the Roman Empire. The important issue for us is that the canon traces the course of imperial rule from the era of Nabonassar, king of Babylon from 747 BC, to the reign of the Roman Emperor Antoninus, 161 AD, presenting four distinct kingdoms. So for Neo-Babylonian, Greek and Roman scholars and historians, the sequence of world history recognises the second world empire as Medo-Persian.

The Book of Daniel certainly presents a joint second empire made up of the Medes and the Persians. Although Daniel states that a Median ruler named Darius supplanted Belshazzar, the last Neo-Babylonian king, there is no reason to doubt that Cyrus the Persian and Darius the Mede were both rulers of the same kingdom simultaneously. When summarising his experience under the new leadership in Babylon, Daniel wrote: 'So Daniel prospered during the reign of Darius and the reign of Cyrus the Persian', an emphatic statement used to describe the joint leadership of the empire.[8]

Non-biblical sources inform us that Daniel's description of a joint kingdom led by two individuals is very precise. The kingdom of Media was absorbed into the Persian kingdom when Cyrus overthrew the Median confederation before the fall of the Neo-Babylonian Empire in 539 BC. The two kingdoms fused together under the leadership of Cyrus into what became the Achaemenid Empire, or The First Persian Empire, named after the more prominent Persian aspect of the empire. However, during the first phase of Cyrus' leadership, the Median half of the empire would have had its own leader, second in command to Cyrus.

Now that a clear case from biblical and non-biblical sources has been presented for understanding the second kingdom to be Medo-Persian, let us turn our attention to its likeness to the silver arms and chest that came after the head of gold in Nebuchadnezzar's dream. In the case of the Neo-Babylonian Empire, the gold represented the political authority of the king - the autocrat and sovereign.

In the case of the Medo-Persian Empire, a clear degradation of political power was present. Cyrus developed a legal framework to which Darius had to submit. This became apparent when the newly appointed Median bureaucrats, jealous of Daniel's promotion over them, cajoled Darius into passing a law which Daniel would have no choice but to disobey. Even when Darius wanted to grant acquittal to Daniel, who had fallen foul of the new law by praying to God, he was unable to do so because of 'the laws of the Medes and the Persians, which cannot be repealed'.[9] As a result, Daniel was thrown into a den of lions, only to be saved by angelic intervention. Clearly Darius was ruling in an oligarchy in which he was bound by higher powers.

Just as gold was a fitting description for the visible aspects of Babylon, so silver was for the Medo-Persian Empire. As we discovered, Nebuchadnezzar brought vast amounts of gold into his kingdom to please the gods. The Medo-Persians brought inordinate amounts of silver into the treasury through taxation, in a manner and fashion that had never happened before, and arguably ever since.

The Medo-Persian Empire was the largest ancient empire. At the height of its power the empire encompassed approximately eight million square kilometres, spanning three continents. Due to its size and the continuous threat from the Assyrians, the entire administration was adapted to cope with these pressures. Daniel informs us that an attempt was made to re-organise the finances of the empire by the appointment of one hundred and twenty Satraps.[10] Although it is unclear whether this new arrangement had a fixed or official tribute for the crown, Herodotus informs us that during the reign of Cyrus and Cambyses, surrounding nations brought many gifts to the king. Furthermore, during the reign of Darius Hystaspes, a system of taxation was perfected across the entire empire. Herodotus records in detail the yearly amount the satrapies of Darius the Mede received each year. The tributes were paid in talents of silver, equating to vast amounts of silver pouring into the Medo-Persian treasury. The only exception in the payment method was that given to the Indians. Due to their large reserves of gold, they were permitted to fulfil their taxation obligations through gold dust, but to the value of four thousand six hundred and eighty talents of silver each year. The fact that the treasury measured gold by the standard and value of silver, provides evidence to demonstrate that silver was the standard for exchange, and the most valued of treasures for the Medo-Persians.

The Medo-Persian lust for silver coinage is also recorded in the Book of Ezra. King Artaxeres was implored by his advisors not to permit the rebuilding of the city of Jerusalem on the basis that once established, it would not continue paying its tribute and taxes to the royal treasury; 'Furthermore, the king should know that if this city is built and its walls are restored, no more taxes, tribute or duty will be paid, and eventually the royal revenues will suffer', (Ezra 4:13). The fact that his advisors used this to deter the king rather than the threat of war or independence from the empire clearly implies that money was the prime motivation of the Medo-Persian rulers. So the chest and arms of silver of the statue in Daniel 2 provide an accurate description of this empire.

The result of taxing such a large empire was that Cyrus and his successors became wealthy. It was revealed to Daniel that the fourth Medo-Persian king, Xerxes, would be far richer than those before him, and through his riches would stir up the realm of Greece, contributing to his downfall, (Daniel 11:2). In 480 BC Xerxes was successful in bridging Hellespont with his army of nearly two million soldiers, and eventually defeated the Spartans at the Battle of Thermopylae leaving a clear route to Athens. However the battle of Salamis in September of the same year

The Final World Empire

proved pivotal for the demise of the Persians and the rise of a united Greek Empire.

The silver aspect of the Medo-Persian Empire is not only confined to the silver chest and arms of the statue of Nebuchadnezzar's dream, but also to the bear-like beast Daniel saw in his night visions.[11] The command the beast was given to 'eat much flesh' could also mean greed and spoliation rather than just conquest and subjugation. In Eastern phraseology, even today, to 'eat' means to 'tax'. Therefore Daniel's vision aptly provides a picture of how this empire pursued silver.

However, the phrase 'eat much flesh' could also have an additional meaning: conquering much territory. If we apply the conquering of vast territories to the Median kingdom, it would make little sense, as it was only after the unification under Cyrus that the empire began to grow and expand considerably. The three ribs in its mouth can then be understood as the three kingdoms it destroyed in its ascension to power in the East: Libya, Babylon and Egypt.

It is also important to remember that this second beast was raised up on one side. Again, this would be an accurate description of what took place in the Medo-Persian Empire. At first, the Median side of the empire was stronger, but during Cyrus' reign, the Persian side outgrew the Median in a very visible way. This further helps us understand that whereas the head of gold in Nebuchadnezzar's statue was a unit, the arms and breast of silver were a duality: two kingdoms combined into one empire.

There is a further piece of evidence to help us with the identity of this second kingdom presented by the Church Father Jerome, writing at the end of the fourth century. During Daniel's dialogue with the angel who came in answer to his supplications in chapter 10, we read of an angelic battle that took place between the messenger and the Prince of Persia, culminating in the assistance of the angel Michael. When Jerome was commenting on this passage, he discovered the word 'Dubiel,' which literally means 'bear-god.'[12] The word was used in the earliest Jewish commentaries on Daniel to identify the Prince of Persia. Likening the angel responsible for the affairs of Persia to a bear-god, is almost an exact description of the second beast that Daniel saw in his vision. Clearly, this second empire was the joint Medo-Persian Empire so often referred to in history.

The Medo-Persian Empire, forged by Cyrus the Great, was destroyed in the Greco-Persian Wars, with its official collapse in 330 BC at the hands of Alexander III of Macedon. This victorious conquest by Alexander the Great over Darius III was revealed to Daniel in advance in a vision, recorded in chapter 8. A goat with a prominent horn travelled from the west with incredible speed and conquered the two-horned ram. The angel Gabriel then informed Daniel that the goat with a prominent horn was the king of Greece who would destroy the Medo-Persian kings represented by the two-horned ram.

---

[7] R. W. Rogers, *Cuneiform Parallels to the Old Testament,* New York, Cincinnati: The Abingdon Press, 1926, pp. 380 ff.

[8] Daniel 6:28.

[9] Daniel 6:12.

[10] Daniel 6:1.

[11] Daniel 7:5.

[12] Jay Braverman, *Jerome's Commentary On Daniel, A study of comparative Jewish and Christian Interpretations of the Hebrew Bible*, The Catholic Biblical Quarterly Monograph Series 7, Washington, America: The Catholic Biblical Association of America, 1978, col. 9.

CHAPTER 5

BRONZE THIGHS AND A FOUR-HEADED LEOPARD

The third phase of the dazzling statue Nebuchadnezzar saw in his night dream was a belly and thighs of bronze. The unique aspect of the Neo-Babylonian Empire was its pagan system of worship, in which lavish amounts of gold were used to pleasure the gods. The sheer territorial dominion of the Medo-Persian Empire made it unique, and the acquisition of silver was the solution to managing the administration that united it. The Greek Empire had numerous aspects that could be deemed unique, but its military strength and technique, which conquered the known world in under a decade, is a worthy candidate for being compared to the bronze belly and thighs of the statue.

Bronze was in fact a unique material that was used extensively by the Grecian Empire in connection with their military. When Herodotus described the armour and uniform of the Grecian warriors during antiquity, he makes frequent reference to 'Grecian Armour'. This armour, first referred to by Homer, a Greek poet in the eighth century BC, was made famous by its use of bronze pieces overlaying the fabric. Whereas the Medes, Persians and Egyptian soldiers wore soft fabric tunics on the day of battle, the Grecian warriors wore muscle-sculpted breastplates, overlaid with bronze. No doubt the reflection in the sun of such ingenious clothing was a formidable sight to their enemies standing on the opposite side of the field, wearing more traditional dress. In fact, there was no other army or people at this time that used bronze in the same way as the Greeks.

Not only was bronze an important component in the military force that swept across the Eastern world, it also became the new standard of monetary exchange in the Greek Empire. The process of issuing bronze coins rather than silver was started in Athens, after the public there started to horde silver coins, removing them from circulation. Just as Ezra referred to the Medo-Persians' quest for silver, the prophet Ezekiel referred to the Greeks using salves and articles of bronze to trade with Tyre for their goods; 'Greece, Tubal and Meshek did business with you; they traded human beings and articles of bronze for your wares.' (Ezekiel 27:13).

The third beast of chapter 7 is a leopard-like creature with four wings and four heads. The combination of a leopard with four wings could be seen to represent an empire that was able to move and conquer quickly, in contrast to the slow-moving bear that preceded it. This is an accurate description of the Greek Empire under Alexander the Great. Whilst still a young man, Alexander not only conquered the world, but did so in such rapid fashion that he will ever be revered as the greatest military commander the world has ever known. In fact, John Calvin said of Alexander that he wept when he heard that there were other worlds that he had not conquered! When Alexander was just thirty-two years of age, his reign was brought to an abrupt and unexpected end by a mysterious disease that claimed his life. Despite dying in his youth, Alexander had conquered the Persian Empire, Egypt and India, making him a military genius and inspiration to later conquerors.

Statue of Alexander the Great in Thessaloniki, Greece

The four heads of the creature that looked like a leopard are descriptive of the political administration of the Greek Empire. Alexander had no obvious or legitimate heir, and strong leadership was needed for this newly birthed empire that bridged the cultures of West

The Final World Empire

and East. Whilst lying on his deathbed, Alexander's companions asked who was to succeed him. Alexander's purported last words of 'to the strongest,' was an open invitation for chaos and instability to be ushered in by warring generals who felt they fitted the dying wish of their leader. After failed attempts to appoint a king who could govern the empire, his four generals, 'The Successors' (*Diadochi*) took power and carved the empire into four areas that became their own independent kingdoms: the Ptolemaic Kingdom of Egypt, the Seleucid Empire in the East, the Kingdom of Pergamon in Asia Minor and the Kingdom of Macedon. The four kingdoms, warring amongst themselves, continued as important factors in world politics until their conquest by the Romans.

So, despite the great military strength of the empire, it began to fragment rapidly due to its politics. Just as the Medo-Persian government was inferior to the Neo-Babylonian, inasmuch that the former was oligarchic – being governed by a small elite group – and the latter was autocratic, the Greek system, in the absence of Alexander, became aristocratic and therefore even weaker. Whereas the Medo-Persians had the rule of a select few, the Greeks had a government led by the nobility. Here blood and family relations were secondary to issues of achievement and success, which could instantly promote someone into the ruling class. The bronze following on from the silver in the statue of chapter 2 clearly shows the deterioration of absolute government and rule.

In Daniel's description of this third world empire, he is informed that 'it was given the authority to rule'.[13] This statement, absent from the other empires, would seem to suggest that God would grant the Greek Empire authority to rule, so that His own plans and purposes might be fulfilled. In a closer look at the politics of the Grecian Empire, it becomes apparent that its weaker politics served to better prepare the world for the coming Messiah.

Greek cities were ruled by leading aristocrats. Before its rapid expansion under Alexander, such aristocrats were themselves Greeks. When the empire crossed the Mediterranean to the east and began to take over towns and cities, the same political system was used. However, rather than leading Greeks presiding over the affairs of the city, it was a fusion of Greek aristocrats being granted new lands in conquered countries and the existing nobility, men of different cultures and religions. Generally speaking, the culture, language and literature of the Greeks were more advanced than the countries it ruled. As a result, those countries and nations that were previously foreign to the Hellenic world, sought to adopt this superior culture in a process now termed *Hellenization*. This contributed to the Greek language, perhaps the most perfect ever devised, becoming the language of the educated, the state, literature, science, traders, the courtier, the government official, the soldier and the traveller. From the time of Alexander, seventy scholars began to translate the Old Testament into Greek, the Septuagint, which enabled the Hebrew Scriptures to permeate the Greek and then Roman worlds. By granting Alexander the decisive victory at the Battle of Gaugamela in 331 BC, resulting in *Hellenization*, it would seem that God was paving the way for His message of salvation to reach every individual in the known world.

After the rule of Alexander the Great, the Greek Empire met conflict from a new emerging force from the west, the Roman Republic. During the third and second centuries BC, Philip V of Macedon and his son Persus, fought Rome in what we now call the Macedonian Wars. Both father and son were defeated in 197 BC and 168 BC respectively. This led to the overall defeat of Macedon, the deposition of the Antigonid dynasty and the dismantling of the Macedonian Kingdom. In 149 BC Roman rule was applied to Macedon and it became the Roman province of Macedonia. The Greek Empire was destroyed, and the Roman Empire held sway over the known world.

However, before we examine the fourth kingdom presented in Daniel 2 and 7, we must momentarily step from the Aramaic section of Daniel and back into the Hebrew by considering chapter 8. In this extraordinary chapter Daniel refers to a development within the third Greek kingdom that would be of disastrous consequence for his people: the ascendance of Antiochus IV Epiphanes. This character proceeds as a leader from the third kingdom who would be a type of final antichrist who will rise from the fourth kingdom at the end of human history. Therefore, we must consider this development next.

---

[13] Daniel 7:6.

CHAPTER 6

THE LITTLE HORNS

We made a brief mention of Daniel's vision of a battle between the goat and the two-horned ram at the end of our examination of the combined Medo-Persian Empire. Gabriel reveals the identity of the goat as being Greece and the two-horned ram as the Medo-Persian Empire.[14] After the victory of the goat, the prominent horn is broken and four horns grow up in its place on the head of the goat. This represents, with astonishing accuracy, the four kingdoms into which Alexander's Empire was divided after his death. Out of one of these horns, another smaller horn appears.

Scholars from both liberal and conservative schools generally agree that the little horn of the goat in Daniel 8 can only refer to Antiochus IV Epiphanes, for no other candidate fits the description as he does. Antiochus IV Epiphanes was eighth in the succession of twenty-six kings in the Syrian division of the Greek Empire. He ruled from 175–164 BC, and sought to expand his kingdom by trying to defeat the Egyptian Pharaohs in the spring of 168 BC. Egypt called on the Romans for assistance, who in turn gave an ultimatum to Antiochus through their representative Gaius Popillius Laenas. Antiochus reluctantly left, and turned his vengeance on Jerusalem. His oppression of the city was twofold. First, he sought to kill as many people of Jewish decent as he could. The Second Book of Maccabees informs us that:

> *Raging like a wild animal, he set out from Egypt and took Jerusalem by storm. He ordered his soldiers to cut down*

> *without mercy those whom they met and to slay those who took refuge in their houses. There was a massacre of young and old, a killing of women and children, a slaughter of virgins and infants. In the space of three days, eighty thousand were lost, forty thousand meeting a violent death, and the same number being sold into slavery.*[15]

This adequately fulfils the interpretation given to Daniel by Gabriel of the attack the little horn would inflict on God's saints.[16]

Antiochus also sought to destroy the Jewish religion. Starting with the temple, Antiochus had the treasures of the holy place taken, and erected an image of Jupiter in their place. A sow was then offered on the altar and its blood scattered over the sanctuary vessels. He substituted the Jewish feasts with the pagan feast of Bacchanalia and forced the Jews left in the city to worship Bacchus, the god of pleasure and wine. Antiochus outlawed the practice of circumcision, killing children who had been circumcised by throwing them off the highest wall in the city with their mothers.

Daniel records that this little horn would: 'set itself up to be as great as the Prince of the host; it took away daily sacrifice from him, and the place of his sanctuary was brought low.'[17] Antiochus was clearly fulfilling this prophecy, setting himself up against God, just as Nimrod had done centuries earlier in Babylon. W.A Criswell speaking of Antiochus, states that he was indeed a foreshadowing of the final antichrist:

> *First, he is inordinately proud, lifted up, and ambitious. He is Satan through copy. He is Satan through incarnation. He is Satan's willing instrument. For example, when Antiochus came to reign, he imprinted on his coins, Theos Antiochus, Theos Epiphanes, "Antiochus, God manifest." One need not doubt that such a thing could be, for according to the second chapter of II Thessalonians, this final dictator presents himself as "God manifest," Theos Epiphanes. That same spirit is universal in human story. Ambitious, dictatorial men are like that. That is the spirit*

> *of Hitler. It is the spirit of any striving dictator who lifts himself above the mountain heap of prostrate humanity.*[18]

The end of the little horn ruler is revealed to Daniel as being a divine act, a visitation of judgement from heaven.[19] Again, we find a correlation to the death of Antiochus IV Epiphanes, who was afflicted with a mysterious and fatal condition of worms and ulcers after declaring war on the Maccabees in 164 BC. The death of King Herod in Acts 12 was also due to an affliction of flesh eating worms, with which the Lord struck him for his failure to attribute praise to God.

Although this little horn would seem similar to the little horn that appears on the fourth beast in Daniel 7, there are numerous differences. Identifying such differences will paint a picture of what the final antichrist of the fourth kingdom will be like.

Whilst receiving the vision of the four beasts, Daniel asks one of those standing within the vision for a clear interpretation.[20] In relation to the fourth beast, with which we are now concerned, Daniel is told that its ten horns are ten kings.[21] After them, a very different king will arise, uprooting three of the kings in his rise to power.[22] Already we now have several differences to the little horn of chapter 8; a different king to his predecessors in comparison to one who had no unique traits; a king who uproots three others as he comes to the throne directly from the head of the beast, in comparison to another who simply arises out of one kingdom. Furthermore, Daniel records personalised traits of the little horn in chapter 7: human eyes and a mouth, whereas no such traits are attributed to the little horn of chapter 8.[23]

In addition, there is a fundamental difference between the two little horns in their relationship to God's people. As we have already noted, the little horn of chapter 8, Antiochus IV Epiphanes, acted directly against the Jewish people and their religion. The king described in chapter 7 on the other hand acts against the 'saints,' a group of people who clearly belong to God, and yet are not linked to any geographical area. The difference between these two distinct groups of people can be seen by the predicted aggression that will be acted against them. To the saints at the mercy of the little horn from the fourth beast in chapter 7, there is a general attack for a three-and-a-half year period of time.[24] However, the people in chapter 8 are subject to the temple functions being taken away.[25]

The resultant punishments for both kings are also very different. Antiochus was removed by a supernatural act of sickness, but the beast from which he sprang is not said to receive any punishment. On the other hand, the king of chapter 7 and his empire face a climactic judgement at the close of world history as the heavenly courtroom is called into place. The saints this king has afflicted receive an eternal kingdom, whereas the people who suffered under Antiochus received no such reward. This eternal kingdom will be universal and fill the whole earth, which is a clear reference to the smiting stone on the feet of the statue of Daniel 2, which grows to become a mountain that fills the whole earth.

Daniel was writing about two very different kings, ruling from two very different empires. If we view the alternation of language used by Daniel to provide his work with a structure, we find another case for concluding that these two kings are not the same. Daniel closes his Aramaic section of the book with the interpretation of the vision of the four beasts in chapter 7, and then reverts to Hebrew at the start of chapter 8 through to the end. This would therefore suggest that the author was closing the section of gentile history in chapter 7, and referring to the events that would befall his own descendants from chapter 8, of which the atrocities caused by Antiochus IV were pivotal.

We can now conclude that the little horn of chapter 7 is a character yet to be revealed. History clearly gives no other viable option. This character will be the final antichrist of a 'revived Roman Empire' at the close of the age. As Martin Luther said: 'in this interpretation and opinion all the world are agreed, and history and fact abundantly establish it.'[26]

---

[14] Daniel 8:20.
[15] Larry Cockerham, "Antiochus IV Epiphanes: The Antichrist of the Old Testament", *Prophecy Forum Home*, < http://prophecyforum.com/ > [accessed 13 Nov 2009].
[16] Daniel 8:24.
[17] Daniel 8:11.

[18] W. Criswell, *Expository Sermons On the Book of Daniel*, Grand Rapids, Michigan: Zondervan Publishing House, 1968, chpt. 4:78.
[19] Daniel 8:25.
[20] Daniel 7:15-16.
[21] Daniel 7:24.
[22] Daniel 7:24.
[23] Daniel 7:20.
[24] Daniel 7:25.
[25] Daniel 8:12.
[26] C. Keil and F. Delitzsch, *Biblical Commentary on the Book of Daniel*, Reprint, Grand Rapids, Michigan: Wm. B. Eerdmans Publishing. Co., 1973, p.245.

CHAPTER 7

IRON MIXED WITH CLAY AND A TERRIFYING BEAST

In Daniel chapter 2, we discover a fascinating difference between the fourth and final empire when compared to the previous three. This empire was described to Nebuchadnezzar as a composition of two materials: iron and clay. Following on from the Greek bronze segment of the statue Nebuchadnezzar saw in his dream, the fourth kingdom would be iron, with its feet being a mixture of iron and clay. Clearly God was showing Nebuchadnezzar that there would be two phases to this final empire, and during its final phase of iron failing to mix with clay, the kingdom of God would literally manifest on the earth bringing destruction to the kingdoms of men.

Just as bronze depicts the Greek military, so iron does of the Roman Empire. Although iron was used to make weapons long before the rise of the Roman Republic, the Greek historian Polybius, writing around 160 BC, described how the Romans were making a landmark shift from bronze to iron in their armoury. The reasons for this are varied, but in part the Roman Republic saw bronze as a substance reminiscent of olden times, not fitting for a republic with ambitions of becoming a global empire.

The Roman soldiers still wore a helmet and breastplate of bronze, but iron was used on their shields, and most importantly on their *pilum*, a new weapon that in part enabled the Roman Empire to conquer the world. A *pilum* could be thrown like a javelin, and its hardened iron tip could penetrate the armour of infantry and horses. Alternatively it could be used as a pike for close combat. The non-hardened iron shank was fastened to a wooden shaft, which meant that when it was driven into a shield, the shank would bend making it impossible to remove, rendering the shield useless. Daniel remarked how the fourth beast he observed in his visions had teeth of iron and claws of bronze. This was no doubt a reference to the mixture of iron and bronze that Polybius recorded the Romans were using.

In Daniel's interpretation of the king's dream it becomes clear that God used iron to reveal a further meaning, one beyond that of the weaponry and outward apparel of the Roman army. Iron spoke of the military strategy of this fourth empire: 'and as iron breaks things to pieces, so it will crush and break all the others', (Daniel 2:4). In the same way, the fourth beast in chapter 7 is said to be different from those before it due to its ability to crush and devour its victims and trample underfoot whatever was left.

Whereas the Grecian Empire absorbed its subjects into its culture and life, the Roman Empire destroyed and replaced whatever civilization would not surrender. The Roman legions seemed to paint an uncompromising line in their war etiquette: surrender would result in emancipation, resistance with annihilation. The destruction of Carthage, the siege of Numantia and the attempted extinction of Jewish nationality during the war against Jerusalem, clearly separated the Roman Empire from the Greek and the Medo-Persian Empires. Josephus records in gruesome detail the fate of Jerusalem in 70 AD at the hands of the Romans, so bent on extermination, that in parts of the city the ground could no longer be seen due to the vast piles of bodies. From the temple sanctuary, where many fled for mercy, the ensuing massacre resulted in a river of human blood flowing from the sanctuary and out from the temple.

The destruction of Jerusalem

This difference in approach to conquest can be attributed in part to the political and philosophical background of the Roman Republic. Although militarily the greatest and most powerful of the world empires, Rome's politics was less autocratic than the previous three, enabling us to apply a third interpretation to the iron used in Nebuchadnezzar's colossus in Daniel 2.

In the early days, the Roman political system was imperialistic, in which the Republic and its visions of dominion and power took precedence over ruler and subjects alike. The First Book of Maccabees records Jewish opinion of the Roman government to which it was subservient:

> *Whomsoever they will to succour and to make kings, these they do make kings; and whomsoever they will, they do depose; and they are exalted exceedingly: and for all this none of them did ever put on a diadem, neither did they clothe themselves with purple, to be magnified thereby.*[27]

For the Jewish people, this was a radical shift from the oriental despotism they had been accustomed to since their captivity in the seventh century BC. In both the Neo-Babylonian and Persian cultures, gentile rulers were elevated to an untouchable plateau far beyond the realm of their subjects, with them alone possessing the ability to choose their successor. However, under Roman occupation, the Jewish nation was now bemused at the sight of rulers being elected on the one hand and deposed by crowds and the mob of Rome on the other.

When Augustus began to transition from republic to empire in 27 BC, he had to do so with powers granted him from the ruling body of the Senate. Amidst these powers to rule, the emperor was granted authority over the military, which in turn guaranteed protection from the Senate. As this empire expanded further from Rome, the weaknesses of such a political system began to manifest. The military failures in Europe gifted the Senate with power once again, and the empire became one of democracy and republics in which the populace had certain rights with regards to the selection of their government.

Due to the Roman policy of citizenship, in which any individual in the empire could purchase Roman citizenship, the governments of the republics were made up of men from different countries and cultures, all seeking different outcomes. The Book of Acts provides a glimpse into the outworking of Roman citizenship when the Apostle Paul appealed to his Roman citizenship for a more balanced trial. This was met by shock and horror by his chief interrogator who had purchased his citizenship at a great cost:

> [25] *As they stretched him out to flog him, Paul said to the centurion standing there, "Is it legal for you to flog a Roman citizen who hasn't even been found guilty?"* [26] *When the centurion heard this, he went to the commander and reported it. "What are you going to do?" he asked. "This man is a Roman citizen."* [27] *The commander went to Paul and asked, "Tell me, are you a Roman citizen?" "Yes, I am," he answered.* [28] *Then the commander said, "I had to pay a lot of money for my citizenship." "But I was born a citizen," Paul replied.* [29] *Those who were about to interrogate him withdrew immediately. The commander himself was alarmed when he realized that he had put Paul, a Roman citizen, in chains.* (Acts 22:25-29)

In an attempt to keep the empire from falling into civil war, Emperor Diocletian in 293 AD changed the constitution of the empire so that it split into four parts, administered by two senior emperors and in association with two Caesars. Although a seemingly radical solution, Diocletian was simply formalising what already existed, which started a process of decentralisation from Rome. The result of this decision was the rise to prominence of other cities, somewhat displacing the role the city of Rome had previously enjoyed. This process of deliberate division did not stop at the empire as a whole, but also in its provinces and in every branch of civil and military administration. Ultimately the empire became one of two halves: the eastern – the Greek territories, now under Roman rule with a capital at Constantinople, and the western – those territories newly conquered and directly answerable to Rome.

Clearly the declining value of the materials used in the statue that Nebuchadnezzar saw in his night dream is a fitting picture of the lessening autocratic power the ruler of each empire had to wield.

In Daniel's final remarks on the statue in chapter 2, he informed Nebuchadnezzar that the fate of this final kingdom was due to its inability to mix the iron and clay together in its feet. This is a picture of the Roman Empire following the policy of division and decentralisation that Diocletian had initiated.

In the West, emperors were never able to either suppress or appease the barbarian tribes. Eventually the barbarian invaders of Goths, Vandals and Huns overran the western territory of Rome, and thereby ended Imperial power in 476 when Romulus Augustus resigned the crown to Odoacer, the first barbarian king of Italy. Although it outlived the Western Roman Empire by nearly one thousand years, the Byzantine Empire faced a similar problem with the Ottoman Turks, a racially and culturally different people group that they were never able to either conquer or absorb into the Roman Empire. Eventually in 1453, Constantinople fell for a second and final time into the Ottoman Empire.

As we now examine this fourth empire from the sub-human perspective from which Daniel viewed it in his night visions, major differences between this beast and the previous three become apparent. First, Daniel is not able to liken it to a wild beast due to its terrifying appearance. Second, the beast has ten horns that represent ten kings (Daniel 7:24). After them a small horn, representing a very different king, would arise, uprooting three of the kings in his rise to power. Furthermore, Daniel records personalised traits of the little horn: human eyes and a mouth.[28] This king would be the final king of the last world empire, standing in opposition to God in a similar manner to that of Nimrod many centuries before.

For a three-and-a-half year period of time this final king acts against the 'saints', a group of people who clearly belong to God, (Daniel 7:25). In response to this aggression, both the king and the fourth beast face judgement at the close of world history as the heavenly courtroom is instituted. The saints this king has afflicted would receive an eternal kingdom, one that is universal and fills the whole earth. This kingdom, which grows to become a mountain that fills the whole earth, is the stone that smashed the feet of the statue in Daniel 2.

There is no evidence to suggest that the little horn that comes from the forth beast has been fulfilled in Roman history. However, the concept of an individual acting in opposition to God can be found in the Roman doctrine of *divi filius*, 'son of the gods.' Just as Nimrod was regarded as a son of the gods in Sumerian religion, and Tamuz after him in the period of the Akkadians, now it was the turn of the Romans to revive this ancient tradition that had begun in Babylon.

In the transition of republic to empire, in 63 BC, Julius Caesar became the *Pontifex Maximus*, the supreme king or priest king. In this new role as head of the state religion, Caesar inaugurated the worship of Venus Genetrix. In this cult, Venus was the mother of Aeneas, who in turn had a son, Iulus. Caesar traced his own origin to Iulus and in doing so laid claim to being a descendent of the gods, which made Venus the divine Mother. However, Julius Caesar had gone too far and his actions offended Rome.

When the laurel crown was placed on Augustus, it was clear that he had masterfully planned how to assume the divine title Julius failed to maintain. In short, Augustus had Julius deified in 42 BC, two years after he died. As his adopted son, Augustus could use the title *divi filius* for himself. Now the scene was set for a divine emperor to advance the Roman Empire across the earth.

The question remains as to the motivation of Julius Caesar to revive a tradition that was birthed in the city of Babylon so many centuries before. Without question, the answer lies in the small city of Pergamon.

Statue of Augustus in Augsburg

Shortly after the arrival of Cyrus in Babylon in 539 BC, the entire Babylonian priesthood travelled northwest and settled in Pergamon.

Despite its elevation to capital of the Pergamene kingdom during the Greek Empire, Pergamon continued the religious practices of the Neo-Babylonians. In 205 BC, whilst Hannibal was in Italy, the Romans learnt from a Sibylline oracle, that Hannibal could be defeated if they brought the Great Mother of the gods from Pessinus in Asia Minor.[29] To do this the Romans required the permission of Attalus I king of Pergamon. Attalus not only granted their request, he facilitated it, enabling the Romans to bring the holiest object, a black meteorite, from the temple of the Great Mother of the gods back to Rome. At almost the same time Roman armies defeated the armies of Hannibal. Naturally, the Great Mother of the gods was worshipped in Rome, and a temple was erected for the worship of the black meteorite under the direction of Claudius. The female deity was named Cybele and the idea of a female mother of gods was fused with the formation of the Roman Republic.

However, it was not only a divine female that Pergamon bestowed on Rome, but also the worship of kings – the sons of gods. On his death in 133 BC, King Attalus III bequeathed the Kingdom of Pergamon to Rome. Although a Hellenistic state, Pergamon preserved this ancient cultic practice of *divi filius*. It was no doubt the acquisition of this knowledge, and the worship of a female mother-god, that allowed Julius Caesar to conceive the idea that he could attribute divinity to himself and his transition from general to emperor. As a result, Pergamon became the home to the Cult of Rome, perpetuating the belief that the Roman emperors were divine.

Statue of Cybele in central Madrid

The deification of the Roman emperors to 'son of the gods' was clearly a satanic work that ran in parallel with the birth of Jesus Christ, the Son of God. Just as Isaiah and the prophets had predicted the arrival of the Jewish Messiah, so too had the Roman writers before Augustus, such as Virgil's fourth Eclogue, in which the Caesars were the Messiahs. Jesus himself informed his disciples that prophetic repetition would occur again in the future before his Second Coming; "Watch out that you are not deceived. For many will come in my name, claiming, 'I am he,' and, 'The time is near.' Do not follow them." (Luke 21:8)

As we considered earlier, this would appear to be a continuation and development of the antichrist spirit inculcated by Antiochus Epiphanes in the Greek Empire.

Not only had this fourth empire produced an antichrist doctrine which emperors could adopt if they wished, the Roman Empire in its infancy persecuted Christians and Jews alike, just as the little horn would do in the future. The Roman senator and historian Tacitus, not writing from a specifically Christian perspective, viewed Roman Emperor Nero as one who sought to extensively torture and execute Christians after the great fire of 64 AD. Emperor Titus six years later laid siege to Jerusalem and entered the city, massacring its inhabitants and destroying the Jewish temple. Josephus claims that one million one hundred thousand people were killed during the siege, of which a majority were Jewish, with a further ninety-seven thousand captured and enslaved.

The events of the Roman emperors carry some similarities to the little horn of Daniel chapter 7, but they are not the same. First, it is impossible in the accounts we have available of the Roman Empire, to find ten successive kings, plus a final king who uproots three contemporaneous kings. Whether one looks at the Roman Empire after its western collapse in 476, or its eastern collapse in 1453, there is no clear list of ten states, kingdoms or nations that are resultant. Second, the vision in Daniel 7 concludes with a divine judgement of this fourth kingdom. As we have already noted, the Roman Empire gradually declined rather than suddenly being stripped of power.

Although we have been able to identify the four kingdoms in Nebuchadnezzar's dream and Daniel's visions as Neo-Babylonian, Medo-Persian, Greek and Roman, there are many who hold to this scheme and yet believe that the fourth kingdom and its final king have already been destroyed by the first advent of Christ, rather than at his Second Coming. To those who hold such a view, the number ten is regarded as symbolic rather than literal. The Romans prophetically repeated the antics and heresies of Antiochus Epiphanes IV in greater measure, all of which furnishes the belief of past fulfilment.

However, a further examination of the climax of the kingdom prophecies in Daniel prove beyond all doubt that the end of the fourth kingdom and arrival of the heavenly kingdom is initiated by the Second Coming of Christ. Furthermore, the angelic visitation to Daniel recorded in chapter 9, reveals a gap of indeterminate time between the death of Jesus and his Second Coming, during which the Roman Empire would have to endure in some form.

---

[27] "1 Maccabees 8, v.13-14", *Art and the Bible*, <http://www.artbible.info/bible/1_maccabees/8.html> [accessed 17 Aug. 2011].

[28] Daniel 7:20.

[29] Sibylline Oracle – a collection of written prophecies attributed to Sibyls, a prophetess in the second century BC.

CHAPTER 8

THE SON OF MAN AND A HEAVENLY KINGDOM

Nebuchadnezzar's dream finished with a rock, cut by supernatural means, colliding with the feet composed of iron and clay. The once formidable statue, representing gentile world history, was smashed so irreparably that the wind blew away the remaining fragments. Daniel informed the king that the stone represented God's kingdom, a fifth and final eternal kingdom that would be the opposite in nature and origin to the four human kingdoms that preceded it. This fifth kingdom has four specific characteristics: it will be established by God, it will never be destroyed, its sovereignty will never be passed on to another people, and it will mark the end of all human kingdoms. This final kingdom would be the one that comes from heaven and fastens itself to earth, thus connecting heaven and earth.

Daniel's vision of the same event from a different perspective in chapter 7 provides an important glimpse of the people who will receive the fifth heavenly kingdom. It is in this personal series of visions that Daniel records an enthronement and judgement scene, which is a typical prophetic picture detailing the end of human history. First, the throne is brought into place for God to take His seat in order to begin His judicial function. This is similar to the account of God that Ezekiel records in chapters 1 and 10. Then, books, plural, are opened to mark the beginning of the court session. There are two biblical references to books to which this phrase is referring. The first is to a record of what individuals have said and done, and the second is a book that contains the names of those who have relationship with God.[30] Judgement is then pronounced on the fourth beast, which is then killed and thrown into the blazing fire, whilst the other three beasts are allowed to live for a time.[31]

At the close of the visions in chapter 7, Daniel describes a character called, 'one like a son of man, coming on the clouds with heaven'.[32] This individual was given glory, authority and sovereign power, attracting worldwide worship and a never-ending kingdom. The one like a son of man hands the fifth and final kingdom to a group of people called 'the saints, the people of the Most High'.

In contrast with the beasts that came from the sea, Daniel saw the Son of Man coming on the clouds of heaven. There are several references in the Old Testament to clouds being an accompaniment of God, and so this individual has a heavenly rather than earthly origin. Furthermore, God leads this character into the courtroom, again suggesting that he is of divine origin.

The fact that Daniel included a comparative preposition in his description of this figure rather than stating 'I saw a man', means that he was only like a man, or more than a man. This Son of Man represents therefore the complete antitype of the little horn of the fourth empire: The Son of Man blesses the saints with a kingdom whereas the little horn uses his kingdom to persecute them. The Son of Man is welcomed into the presence of God, whereas the little horn faces eternal judgement.

When Jesus Christ began his ministry nearly six hundred years after the life and work of Daniel, his use of this title 'Son of Man' would suggest that this passage in Daniel 7 is Messianic. The authors of the New Testament Gospels record Christ using this term seventy-eight times in their literary accounts of his life and ministry. Jesus did not compare himself to the Son of Man in Daniel; he claimed that he was that person! Apart from the possibility of using this title to emphasise his humanity, there can be little evidence to suggest why Jesus should use this title, other than showing he was the fulfilment of the vision from Daniel 7.

This does not answer the question over which advent of Christ fulfils the prophecy of the stone striking the feet of the image, or of the Son of Man passing the final kingdom to God's people.

The Final World Empire

In the same way Jesus was emphatic over his identity as the Son of Man, his teachings make plain that Daniel 2 and 7 were referring to his second advent. In the Olivet discourse Jesus informed his disciples that after the days of great distress that mark the end of the age:

> *Men will see the Son of Man coming on the clouds with great power and glory. And he will gather his elect from the four winds, from the ends of the earth to the ends of the heavens. (Mark 13:26-27)*

Here in two verses, the climax of biblical eschatology is realised: Jesus returns from heaven and sends his angels to gather his elect people from heaven and earth. This is a clear reference to the closing scene in Daniel 7. Jesus again describes himself as the divine Son of Man that Daniel saw coming on the clouds of heaven.

The role of the angels in gathering the elect concludes Jesus' specific teaching on the role of angels at the end of the age. In the Parable of the Sower, Jesus explained that angels are the harvesters of souls, separating God's people from Satan's people. This same role unfolds further in the Parable of the Weeds which Matthew records immediately after the Parable of the Sower. Here, Jesus told his disciples in a private setting that the angels will perform this gathering function at the final harvest at the end of the age.[33] Those not belonging to God are punished, whilst the righteous elect 'shine like the sun in the kingdom of their Father'.[34] Such clear and intentional references to Christ's Second Coming, the final gathering for judgement and a kingdom for his elect, provides a precise explanation of the judgement scene in Daniel 7.

The teaching of Christ also helps us differentiate between the spiritual arrival of his kingdom at the time of John the Baptist and a future physical arrival of his kingdom on earth at his Second Coming. At the Passover feast before his death, Jesus informed his disciples that they would one day sit on thrones in heaven judging the twelve tribes of Israel.[35] This was one of their roles in the new kingdom that Christ had conferred on them; the same kingdom his Father had given to him.[36] Again, Jesus was clearly referring to the judgement scene in Daniel 7;

thrones are mentioned in both, the kingdom is passed from God to Christ and from Christ to his saints, with judgment following.

If the Second Advent of Jesus marks the entrance of the fifth kingdom, the one it replaces must be the final human empire led by an antichrist figure. As a result, this interpretation of the eschatological elements of the dream of Daniel 2 and the vision of chapter 7 gives a place for a future expectation of a 'Roman Empire', from which, or in response to which, a final antichrist figure will arise.

This was the view of some of the Early Church Fathers, believing that the fulfilment of the final stages of the prophecies in Daniel 2 and 7 would be a future event, initiated by the return of Jesus Christ. The most notable Church Father in this regard was Irenaeus of Lyon, priest and author during the reign of Marcus Aurelius, emperor of Rome in the later part of the second century. He stated that Rome was a prophetic kingdom that would end in a tenfold partition and so fulfilling the ten horns of the fourth beast in Daniel 7. Although the temple had been destroyed in 70 AD by the Romans, Irenaeus believed that there would be a prophetic repetition – the temple being rebuilt where the antichrist, a Roman ruler, would enthrone himself in fulfilment of Daniel's prophecy of the little horn in chapter 7. This would last for three and a half years, based on his understanding of Daniel 9, and would be immediately followed by the Second Coming of Christ.

At this stage we have built a clear case for expecting a future 'Roman Empire' of some kind from which the antichrist will arise before Jesus returns, which concurs with the consensus view of the Early Church Fathers. However, before we consider the demise of the Roman Empire and any subsequent 'revivals' of this empire, we must answer the important question over the gap in time between the official collapse of the Roman Empire and return of Christ. Does Daniel provide us with any evidence that would suggest that the fourth empire would endure in some form or other over the succeeding two thousand years until the return of Jesus?

---

[30] Exodus 32:32; Psalms 69:28; Malachi 3:16; Psalms 56:8-9; Psalms 139:16.
[31] Daniel 7:11-12.

[32] Daniel 7:13.
[33] Matthew 13:30.
[34] Matthew 13:43.
[35] Luke 22:28-30.
[36] Luke 22:29.

CHAPTER 9

THE GAP

It has been the failure to provide a clear biblical case for the gap in time from the Roman Empire to the present day, currently standing at over two millennia, that has led to numerous publications relegating the prophecies of Daniel to past fulfilment during either the Greek or Roman empires. However, a closer examination of subsequent prophetic insights Daniel received during his ministry in Babylon, serve to prove that the case for such a gap is entirely acceptable. Furthermore, such insights add depth to the arguments and conclusions that we have already established.

In 539 BC, the first year of the reign of Darius the Mede, king of Babylon, Daniel read the scroll of Jeremiah and made the startling discovery that Jerusalem would be subject to Babylonians for the duration of their empire: 'This is what the Lord says: "When seventy years are completed for Babylon, I will come to you and fulfil my good promise to bring you back to this place."' (Jeremiah 29:10). Historians largely agree that the ascendancy of the Neo-Babylonian Empire was marked by the defeat of the Assyrian Empire at Haran in 609 BC, exactly seventy years prior to Darius the Mede's reign in Babylon. When he realised the significance of Jeremiah's words, Daniel commenced to pray fervently on behalf of his nation.[37]

Readers of Daniel 9 then discover the greatest 'interruption' to prayer that has ever taken place; the archangel Gabriel appeared with a message! The message, or rather prophecy, concerned the precise timeframe for the events that would mark the climax of biblical prophecy.

A period of seventy 'sevens' had been decreed for Daniel's people in which six specific events would take place: the finish of transgression; the ending of sin; an atonement for wickedness; the arrival of everlasting righteousness; the sealing up of vision and prophecy; and the anointing of the Holy Place.[38]

This period of seventy weeks is held by commentators to mean four hundred and ninety years, made up of seventy lots of seven-year periods. Just as Daniel had understood that the Neo-Babylonian Empire would endure and dominate Mesopotamia for seventy years, God was showing him that the entire history of Israel would be consummated in a period of seventy 'sevens' of years.

Although for a Western mind it may at first seem a strange method of communicating four hundred and ninety years, translators used the word 'weeks' due to our understanding and use of a seven-day week. Gabriel was therefore splitting the four hundred and ninety years into units of seven. Clearly this would have meant for Daniel that this was not to be a continuous and unbroken period of time. Interestingly, a basketball game provides us with a clear example of how we are to understand this. The match lasts for forty-eight minutes, and yet those minutes are not continuous; timeouts, fouls and other aspects suspend play. Often, the forty-eight minutes takes place in sections that total over an hour and a half.

To add detail to the four hundred and ninety years represented as seventy weeks, Gabriel informed Daniel that they are split into three separate periods of time. The first is a period of seven weeks, or forty-nine years, initiated by a command given to rebuild Jerusalem.[39] The second is a period of sixty-two weeks, or four hundred and thirty-four years, after which the Anointed One will be cut off and the sanctuary will be destroyed.[40] The final third period of time of one week or seven years is of special interest, because Gabriel divides this into two three-and-a-half year periods.[41] In the first period, the final world ruler will declare a covenant with the Jewish people and restore temple worship. In the second period, the covenant is broken and worship in the temple by the Jewish people ceases until some divine agent destroys the ruler.[42] Now let us consider each of these three periods of time.

Gabriel clearly states: 'Know and understand this: From the time the word goes out to restore and rebuild Jerusalem...'[43] The clear emphasis is on the rebuilding of Jerusalem and refers to the decree of King Artaxerxes Longimanus to Nehemiah on 14 March 445 BC.[44] The Book of Nehemiah provides a beautiful account of the providence of God in restoring the fortunes of Jerusalem, and using the cupbearer of the king to initiate such an historic turn of events.

King Artaxerxes grants freedom to the Jews

When we add to this date the first unit of time, forty-nine years, we arrive at 396 BC. During this time both the temple and the walls of Jerusalem had been built just as Gabriel had predicted; 'It will be rebuilt with streets and a trench, but in times of trouble', (Daniel 9:25).

In 396 BC the second period of sixty-two 'sevens' or four hundred and thirty-four years started. Using the basis of a three hundred and sixty day year, provided by the biblical references to years in Genesis and Revelation, this equates to one hundred and fifty-six thousand two hundred and forty days, and takes us to 6 April 32 AD. Gabriel had informed Daniel that this period would end with 'the Anointed One' being cut off and having nothing (Daniel 9:26). On 6 April 32 AD, Jesus rode on a donkey from Bethany, where he had been anointed for his burial, to Jerusalem, fulfilling Zechariah 9:9: 'Rejoice greatly, Daughter Zion! Shout, Daughter Jerusalem! See, your king comes to you, righteous and victorious, lowly and riding on a donkey, on a colt, the foal of a donkey.' On his arrival in Jerusalem the people hailed Christ as the Messiah, or anointed one, using Psalm 118.

Despite the precise fulfilment of Gabriel's prophecy to Daniel, Luke records the failure of the people to recognise the significance of the day and the consequent pain this caused Jesus:

> *⁴¹ As he approached Jerusalem and saw the city, he wept over it ⁴² and said, "If you, even you, had only known on this day what would bring you peace—but now it is hidden from your eyes. ⁴³ The days will come upon you when your enemies will build an embankment against you and encircle you and hem you in on every side. ⁴⁴ They will dash you to the ground, you and the children within your walls. They will not leave one stone on another, because you did not recognize the time of God's coming to you." (Luke 19:41-44)*

Jesus knew that he was to be cut off from his people through death and would be assigned a grave outside the city. What is even more remarkable is that Jesus then adds detail to the next part of Gabriel's prophecy, by explaining what would happen in the Jewish war against the Romans. Gabriel had informed Daniel that: 'The people of the ruler who will come will destroy the city and the sanctuary.' (Daniel 9:26). Thirty-eight years later Titus Vespasian with four Roman Legions laid siege to the city, and after nine months, in 70 AD, overran and destroyed the city.

So far, we can see that Gabriel's prophecy was fulfilled with miraculous precision. Let us now consider the final period of time of which Gabriel spoke:

> *²⁶ After the sixty-two 'sevens,' the Anointed One will be put to death and will have nothing. The people of the ruler who will come will destroy the city and the sanctuary. The end will come like a flood: War will continue until the end, and desolations have been decreed. ²⁷ He will confirm a covenant with many for one 'seven.' In the middle of the 'seven' he will put an end to sacrifice and offering. And at the temple he will set up an abomination that causes desolation, until the end that is decreed is poured out on him. (Daniel 9:26-27)*

The second period of time, four hundred and thirty-four years, concludes with the death of Jesus Christ. The destruction of the city and the temple occur after this period in 70 AD. Interestingly, Gabriel points out that the final antichrist would be a descendent of those Roman Legions that sacked Jerusalem in 70 AD, giving further evidence of a future 'revived Roman Empire'. Gabriel then proceeds to speak of the tumultuous times that lie ahead before the start of the final seven-year period. So whereas Gabriel purposely stated that the first two periods of time were successive, here he indicates a gap, the one in which we are now living. This will be found to be correct as we consider in detail what will take place in the final period of time.

Gabriel closes the final period of world history by stating how the ruler who will come, will 'set up an abomination that causes desolation.' This suggests that the temple in Jerusalem, destroyed by the Romans in 70 AD, must be rebuilt so that future sacrifices and offerings can be stopped for this abomination to take place. As referred to earlier, in the Olivet discourse Jesus revealed how the temple in Jerusalem would be despoiled as in the time of Antiochus Epiphanes, and then destroyed, which would be followed by his return.[45] By using the same terminology of 'the abomination that causes desolation', Jesus can be said to be referring to the seventy weeks of Daniel. Therefore, the destruction of the temple in 70 AD was in fact a foreshadowing of some future event that a descendent of the Roman Empire would initiate. The period of time in-between can therefore be of any length. There is now growing evidence to suggest that Israelis are seeking to rebuild the temple in Jerusalem. When such work is complete, we can be sure that the scene is set for the final seven years of history.

---

[37] Daniel 9:4-19.
[38] Daniel 9:21-24.
[39] Daniel 9:25.
[40] Daniel 9:25.
[41] Daniel 9:26.
[42] Daniel 9:27.
[43] Daniel 9:25.
[44] This date and the following interpretation of the seventy 'weeks' use the Julian calendar.
[45] Mark 13.

CHAPTER 10

THE FOURTH BEAST IN THE NEW TESTAMENT

'The new is in the old concealed; the old is in the new revealed'. This beautiful statement made by Saint Augustine expresses the intimate relationship between the testaments. In order to understand the New Testament, one must know the Old Testament. So having considered the fourth empire in the Old Testament, we can now turn our attention to the stunning revelation given to John, the disciple of Christ, during his exile on Patmos at around 96 AD. In the Book of Revelation chapters 13 and 17, John records in extraordinary detail the activity and destiny of the fourth empire at the close of world history. A thorough examination of both chapters, in the light of what we already know about the fourth empire, will enable us to add the final brush strokes to our portrait of the final world empire at the close of human history.

Revelation 13 - The Dragon, the Beast from the Sea and the Beast from the Earth

The thirteenth chapter of the Apocalypse presents three characters: a dragon, a beast from the sea, and a beast from the earth. In the previous chapter, Satan is revealed as the dragon seeking to devour the male child of a woman.[46] Having failed in this mission, the dragon stands by the sea as the two beasts appear. John learns that the beast from the earth is a false prophet who works in partnership with the beast from the sea.[47] The ten horns, blasphemous words, and persecution of God's people for a period of three-and-a-half years, can leave us in no doubt that the beast from the sea is the same terrible fourth beast that Daniel saw in his night visions. This beast we have identified as the Roman Empire.

Interestingly, there are several distinct and important differences between the two beasts. The beast John saw rising from the sea had the outward attributes from each of the four beasts revealed to Daniel, but in reverse order. His beast resembled a leopard, but had feet like those of a bear, and had the mouth like that of a lion. We know that the leopard represents the Greek Empire, the bear the Medo-Persian Empire and the lion the Neo-Babylonian Empire. In addition, here in the Book of Revelation, the beast from the sea has seven heads - the sum total of the heads of all four beasts that Daniel had seen previously. In light of this, it would seem that John was viewing the final 'revived Roman Empire' as both a continuation of the previous empires and a coalescence of all previous satanic forces into one unit that would ultimately be judged by God.

The other significant difference here is that John was privy to seeing the fourth world empire in its final form as both a kingdom and an individual. In fact, all three characters in Revelation 13 are personified. We have already identified the dragon as Satan, and we discover in Revelation 16 that the beast that rises from the earth is the false prophet.[48] The beast from the sea is none other than the antichrist. Together in John's vision, the devil, the antichrist and false prophet represent a type of satanic trinity.

This presentation of the final world empire as a person will become even more emphatic when we consider Revelation 17. However, there is a striking parallel found in King Nebuchadnezzar's dream of the statue in Daniel 2. When interpreting the dream, Daniel informed the pagan king that he was the head of gold and yet, at the same time, the head of gold was the Neo-Babylonian Empire. So here, in the revelation given to John, we understand that the Roman Empire will span the course of history and will ultimately rest upon one individual – the antichrist.

The dragon, or Satan, is the instigative agent behind the beast from the sea. John explains that the dragon gave the beast 'his power and his throne and great authority', in a similar manner to how God the Father bestowed such rewards on His son.[49] The parallels between the Christ and the antichrist extend further when John informs us that a seemingly fatal wound on one of the heads of the beast was miraculously healed. This grand miracle brought acclamation to the beast from the masses who were 'filled with wonder' and started to follow the beast.[50] In the same way, Christ was fatally wounded – wounded to the death, being revealed to John as a lamb that had been slain and yet is alive.[51] This theme of death and resurrection, since its cultic inception in Babylon after Nimrod's death, can now be expected not only in subsequent 'revivals' of the 'Roman Empire', but also in its ruler. Just as Jesus was born, died and rose again during the Roman Empire through the agency of God, so this empire and its antichrist rulers would die and be resurrected by the agency of the dragon.

This principal of multiple, temporary, and yet future appearances of the antichrist is found in Paul's second letter to the church in Thessalonica, and also in John's epistles. Paul refers to the antichrist as the 'man of lawlessness' who would come in the future, but warns the church that the mystery of lawlessness was already at work in the form of false teachings.[52] Paul teaches that his demise would come when Christ returns at his Second Coming accompanied by his followers.[53] Just as the little horn of the Greek Empire in Daniel 8 was a type of antichrist, we can anticipate that subsequent 'revivals' of the 'Roman Empire' will feature such figures. But more importantly, the little horn of the fourth beast in Daniel 7 becomes analogous to the final empire that John saw in his vision.

For John, the message of resurrection in the apocalyptic scenes was alarmingly relevant to his own immediate plight. Having been exiled to Patmos by Emperor Domitian around 96 AD, John would have been familiar with Nero-*redivivus*, the legend that Emperor Nero would be miraculously raised to life and wreak revenge on Rome. During the time of Domitian there was a candidate acting as the resurrected emperor who brought fear to both Romans and Christians. For the former, such an individual could cause civil war, whilst for the church, Nero stood as a type of antichrist due to his vehement persecution of Christians.

Furthermore, the vision of John in Revelation 13 provides insight to the intentions of Satan, which in turn will assist us as we address likely candidates for being classified as a 'revival' of the 'Roman Empire'. The first is the desire to receive worship: 'People worshipped the dragon because he had given authority to the beast, and they also worshipped the beast and asked, "Who is like the beast? Who can wage war against it?"'[54] Here Satan uses incomparability to receive the worship of men. By causing the final empire and its antichrist ruler to have supreme and seemingly matchless power, mankind would have nothing with which to compare it and so worship its originator. Just as the antichrist beast imitates Jesus the Lamb, Satan here imitates God who is frequently worshipped in the Old Testament because of His incomparability.[55]

In the same way as the fourth beast in Daniel's night vision began to speak 'boastfully' and 'oppress the saints' for 'a time, times and half a time', so the beast from the sea 'was given a mouth to utter proud words and blasphemies and to exercise its authority for forty-two months.'[56] The dragon is not credited for giving the beast his mouth or the three-and-a-half year time frame in which to act. Perhaps of great comfort to John was the knowledge that God is clearly in control of both the activity and schedule of the antichrist so that His own purposes would be fulfilled.

To leave us in no doubt that John was viewing the same final period of three-and-a-half years that Daniel first saw in connection to the fourth beast, which Gabriel later elaborated on, we are informed that the antichrist will explicitly 'blaspheme God' and 'slander his name and his dwelling-place and those who live in heaven.'[57] Once again, we have a reference to God's dwelling place - the temple in Jerusalem. The Apostle Paul describes this same activity in his teaching to the Thessalonians about the antichrist: 'He will oppose and will exalt himself over everything that is called God or is worshipped, so that he sets himself up in God's temple, proclaiming himself to be God.'[58]

However, in John's closing description of the beast, we ascertain an important additional insight about the power of the antichrist and his empire at the close of world history:

> [7] *It was given power to wage war against God's holy people and to conquer them. And it was given authority over every tribe, people, language and nation.* [8] *All inhabitants of the*

> *earth will worship the beast – all whose names have not been written in the Lamb's book of life, the Lamb who was slain from the creation of the world.' (Revelation 13:7-8)*

Whereas Daniel foresaw power and dominion over God's people, John reveals the extent and reach of the beast's power. The antichrist and final world empire will not have jurisdiction over Israel alone, but over every people group on earth. The result of such power, as aforementioned, will be that every person who does not have a relationship with Jesus Christ will worship the antichrist.

As we now turn to yet a further vision of the beast in the Book of Revelation, let us summarise the four additional characteristics that we can anticipate in the final world empire. John's retrospective view of previous three world empires, and the activity of the final world empire, suggests an unbroken succession of 'revived' empires from the collapse of the ancient Roman Empire until the final manifestation. Second, the final world empire will be established by and governed by the antichrist. The identification of the empire with the antichrist means that the recurring antichrist theme of death and resurrection can be applied not only to the historic Roman Empire, but also to an individual. And finally, the 'revived Roman Empire' will achieve that which its historic counterpart failed to do: dominion and governance over the West as well as the East. Such a universal system of government will satisfy Satan's chief aim of receiving worship from mankind, who is made in the image of God.

Revelation 17 - The Woman Riding the Beast

In Revelation 17 John records, with great astonishment, the curious sight of a woman straddling the beast that has seven heads and ten horns. It is this vision, along with Gabriel's prophecy in Daniel 9, that have been perhaps the most frequently debated texts relating to eschatology in the Bible. A correct understanding of this vision will be critical for our study as we seek to anticipate the final world empire and the antichrist in the form of a 'revived Roman Empire.' We will consider the characters of this vision in Revelation 17, and the details attributed to them, in the sequence the angel revealed them to John.

John is invited to witness 'the punishment of the great prostitute, who sits by many waters.'[59] The description of the woman being a prostitute is a continuation of an Old Testament theme in which a prostitute was symbolic for those who actively lead the innocent from the right path into deception, mainly through idolatry. The activity of the prostitute with the 'kings of earth' and the resultant intoxication that befell them introduces an economic theme – a theme that the angel would soon expound to John in greater detail.

The woman that John saw is Babylon. The reference to the 'many waters' is descriptive of Babylon due to its situation between the Euphrates and the Tigris rivers. Jeremiah refers to Babylon as the city of 'many waters', and the Israelites sang their famous Psalm about Zion whilst sitting by the 'rivers of Babylon' during their exile.[60] The fusion of religious and economic perversion is also an apt portrayal of the ancient city. Nimrod founded Babylon upon the ideology that man was equal to God, and therefore prosperity and wealth could be achieved without any need for divine intervention; rather, man would be far happier and wealthier without God! As we have already seen in our brief overview of history since the rise of the Neo-Babylonian Empire, the kings of the earth all too gladly drank from the cup of Babylon.

The Old Testament explicitly refers to three other nations as being prostitutes like Babylon; with these John would have been familiar. The first of course is Israel, repeatedly being referred to as an unfaithful wife and prostitute due to her idolatry for financial reward.[61] Similarly, both Tyre and Nineveh are presented by the prophets Ezekiel, Isaiah and Nahum as being harlots for turning back to idolatry from the salvation they had received.[62]

Here in John's vision, Babylon is reserved for God's ultimate judgement for being found responsible for producing the wine that caused such nations to fall victim of deception. Both Isaiah and Hosea reveal how spiritual drunkenness causes numbness and blindness.[63] Once drunk, nations are powerless to resist Babylon's destructive influence and become numb to any notion that God's judgement might be pending. Tyre and Nineveh stand as powerful witnesses to the gentile world of nations who received salvation, and all the blessings that accompany redemption, and yet turned back to idol worship and the economic oppression of the nations around them.

After John's initial introduction to the woman, the angel carried the prophet to the desert where he saw the prostitute 'sitting on a scarlet beast that was covered with blasphemous names and had seven heads and ten horns.'[64] Although in the initial description John is told that the woman is located in Babylon, John now sees her riding the beast from the sea – the final stage of the 'Roman Empire' and the antichrist. To leave us in no doubt that the woman is straddling a 'revived Roman Empire', we learn that the woman is sat on the seven heads of the beast, which are also 'seven hills'. Only two cities can match this literal description of being founded on seven hills: Rio de Janeiro and Rome. However, the latter has been referred to as a city on seven hills for well over two thousand years and is still referred to as such today.

During our study of Daniel's fourth empire, we discovered that the Caesars expediently used the ancient ideals of Babylon during the transition from republic to empire. In fact, Rome shared so many parallels to Nimrod's ancient city that John's countrymen often referred to Rome as 'Babylon.' Clearly Rome had drunk from the woman's cup and had even followed her ancient narrative by destroying the temple in Jerusalem and persecuting God's people.

The woman John saw was both the literal city of Babylon – situated by 'many waters', and the spirit of Babylon that was dominating the formation of the Roman Empire. This dual identity of the woman becomes apparent when John turned his attention to her outward attire: 'The woman was dressed in purple and scarlet, and was glittering with gold, precious stones and pearls. She held a golden cup in her hand, filled with abominable things and the filth of her adulteries.'[65] The items adorning her scarlet dress are referred to in Revelation 18 as products of trade that made Babylon prosperous. However, such objects also presented a further religious meaning. John was familiar with the clothing of the High Priest, which the Septuagint presents as gold, purple, scarlet, linen and precious stones. Furthermore, during a period of prostitution, Israel spiritually wore these same garments to seduce her lovers.[66] The spirit of Babylon was both religious and economic in nature, with the ability to straddle a literal political empire.

John's personal astonishment at the vision of the woman riding the beast reached a climax when he saw her persecution of 'God's holy people' and saw her name emblazoned upon her forehead, 'MYSTERY BABYLON THE GREAT THE MOTHER OF PROSTITUTES AND OF THE ABOMINATIONS OF THE EARTH'.[67] Throughout the Book of Revelation, people are presented with a name on their forehead with the purpose of expressing their true identity as either belonging to God, or to Satan. Here, the prostitute's true identity is unveiled to John as 'Babylon the great', the very same terminology King Nebuchadnezzar used whilst walking on the roof of the royal palace in Babylon: 'Is not this the great Babylon I have built as the royal residence, by my mighty power and for the glory of my majesty?'[68] Daniel informs us that while these words were still on the lips of the proud king, judgement came from heaven. In the very same way, John is soon to learn of a heavenly judgement on this proud woman.

The prefix of 'MYSTERY' also finds interpretation through the Book of Daniel. Each of Daniel's visions was also a mystery. Each world empire appeared as part of a magnificent statue, and also as wild beasts rising from the sea. More importantly, Babylon was a person and an empire. As we have just considered here and previously, the mystery concerning Nebuchadnezzar was dramatically fulfilled through a divine infliction of mental derangement. Later, Daniel interpreted the mysterious writing on the wall in the presence of King Belshazzar, which marked the dramatic end of the Neo-Babylonian Empire: 'That very night Belshazzar, king of the Babylonians, was slain, and Darius the Mede took over the kingdom, at the age of sixty-two.'[69] In the same way, John was viewing this woman as a duality at the end of her reign: the literal city of Babylon and spirit of Babylon in the form of a pagan economic and religious system.

It is perhaps the economic and religious activities of the prostitute that claim the lives of so many of 'God's holy people… those who bore testimony to Jesus.'[70] Just as the prophet Daniel had faced the threat of execution on numerous occasions whilst living in Babylon for refusal to worship the deity of the day, Christians living in first century Asia

Minor faced enormous pressure to pay homage to gods of the trade guilds and to the Roman emperor. Those who failed to participate in such homage were economically ostracised. This interpretation is consistent when we consider the work of the beast from the earth, the false prophet, who will demand that the inhabitants of the earth must 'receive a mark on their right hands or on their foreheads, so that they could not buy or sell unless they had the mark, which is the name of the beast or the number of its name.'[71]

However, amidst such persecution, John views an abrupt and somewhat ironic end to the woman. God turns the beast and the ten horns upon which she is seated against her. In the end, they 'will bring her to ruin and leave her naked; they will eat her flesh and burn her with fire.'[72] The antichrist and the political and military side of his empire will turn against the religious and economic side and prove victorious. Although such a sequence of events would appear to hale the division of Satan's kingdom, the opposite is in fact the case.

As we discovered in our examination of the beast from sea, Satan's chief intention is to receive worship from mankind. In the religious and economic system that Nimrod first introduced in Babylon, man ultimately worshipped himself in defiance of God. The Tower of Babel is a clear outward manifestation of this. However, in the very last moments of human history, during the three-and-a-half years, Satan will remove his veil and demand worship for himself. For this to happen, Babylon would have to be destroyed so that mankind is exclusively dependent upon Satan for prosperity.

The location in which the judgement against the woman takes place provides us with a further insight to the activities of the antichrist and the 'revived Roman Empire' at the close of world history. In the angel's closing words to John, the woman is situated back on the 'waters' and is once again referred to as 'the great city that rules over the kings of the earth.'

Such judgement being poured upon the literal city of Babylon is spoken of throughout the Old Testament, and also in the very next chapter of the Book of Revelation. Those who fail to note the dual aspects of the prostitute's identity have no adequate method for explaining this destruction. This is in part because both Isaiah and Jeremiah speak with clinical accuracy about the details of Babylon's destruction, which has not yet happened at any point in history. Jeremiah reveals how the city would become uninhabitable, with even the stones being unsafe for building. Isaiah connects the destruction of Babylon with the final judgement by God at the close of human history. Since the fall of Babylon into the hands of Medo-Persians, Babylon has always been inhabited, and is home to many this very day. In the early 1980's, Saddam Hussein used original stones in an attempt to rebuild parts of ancient Babylon. Clearly a future judgement awaits the literal city, just as it does the spiritual.

There is yet further evidence to support the angel's message to John of a specific location at which both spiritual Babylon and literal Babylon will be destroyed. Zechariah, writing just after the conquest of the Neo-Babylonian Empire, had a vision of a woman, imprisoned in a lead basket, being taken back to 'the country of Babylonia to build a house for it.'[73] We can be in no doubt that the 'country of Babylonia', or 'Shinar', refers to the city of Babylon in modern day Iraq. Just as the great prostitute of Revelation 17 was guilty of influencing the kings of the world with the wine of her adulteries, so Zechariah learnt that this woman in the basket was called 'Wickedness'. Clearly, the spirit of Babylon, which throughout history has influenced the entire world, will ultimately arrive back in the city of Babylon to face divine judgement.

When we consider possible 'revivals' of the 'Roman Empire' in more recent history, we can anticipate a religious and economic system typified by the harlot of Revelation. However, let us finally turn our attention to the details John records of the beast and his ten horns.

Just as Daniel required wisdom to understand King Nebuchadnezzar's dreams of the colossus representing the four successive world empires, the angel informs John that a 'mind of wisdom' is needed to understand the seven heads of the beast. Again we find a double meaning. On the one hand they are 'seven hills on which the woman sits', which we have identified as Rome. The angel then proceeds to reveal that they 'are also seven kings.'[74] Furthermore, five kings had already come, the sixth king was present at the time of the vision, and a seventh would come but for 'only a little while.' Finally, the beast itself is revealed as the eighth king who 'once was, and now is not.'[75]

In order to follow the instruction of the angel, we should adopt the method that Daniel used for interpreting such apocalyptic scenes – receiving a heavenly endowment of wisdom! Daniel consistently differentiated between the heads of beasts and the horns of beasts when interpreting his visions. The heads could either be individuals who embodied the empire the beast represented, or kingdoms of the empire. Horns on the other hand were always sovereign individuals.

By stating that the sixth king was present at the time of the prophecy, we can be in no doubt that this was a reference to the Roman Empire rather than a particular Roman emperor. No matter how creatively one counts the succession of Roman emperors, and many have undertaken the arduous task of doing so, it is impossible to produce a list of six to the time of John's exile around 96 AD. Clearly the seven heads of the beast are world empires seen by John here as a single unit. This is made clearer when we consider that the eighth king will be one of the seven kings and yet the beast itself. The antichrist will be the enigmatic individual upon whom the 'revived Roman Empire' will rest and thus be the beast itself.

If we start from the sixth head being the Roman Empire, and work backwards through the kingdom scheme set out by Daniel, we arrive at the third head being the Neo-Babylonian Empire. But what of the other two heads? The answer to this question again lies in the prompting of the angel to remind John of the wisdom that Daniel sought. Although history presents many significant ancient empires prior to the Neo-Babylonian that could be considered, Daniel understood that the lens through which God was revealing world history was that of the nation of Israel. All four empires presented by Daniel played a profound role in the nation of Israel and the people of God. As God sought to show Daniel what would happen next, revelation began with Nebuchadnezzar. However, the Old Testament provides great detail about two other empires that formed part of God's divine plan and intention for the nation of Israel: Egypt and then Assyria. For John, the picture of world empires acting in defiance of God and His people would not be complete without Egypt and Assyria being somehow represented. And so here the sovereignty of God to John and the Jewish people is seen.

The seventh king or empire is of particular interest to our study. Firstly, we know from our investigation of Daniel that the final empire was Roman, which would somehow endure or undergo a series of 'revivals' until the end of time. Secondly, the angel here describes the seventh king or empire as only remaining for 'a little while', just as the feet of the statue in Daniel 2 fail to cleave to one another. If we consider this along with the death and resurrection of one of the seven heads that John observed in the previous revelation, we find a reference to anticipated death and resurrection of the Roman Empire beyond that of its literal collapse. This seventh head can therefore refer to numerous 'revivals' of the 'Roman Empire' until the climax of the eighth and final manifestation – one that is made unique by the appearance of the antichrist.

In the light of the conclusions we have made so far, we can now explore when and where this seventh head, or 'revived Roman Empire' has occurred following the official collapse of the Roman Empire.

---

[46] Revelation 12:4.
[47] Revelation 16:13; 19:20; 20:10.
[48] Revelation 16:3.
[49] Revelation 13:2.
[50] Revelation 13:3.
[51] Revelation 5:6.
[52] 2 Thessalonians 2:2-3, 7.
[53] 2 Thessalonians 2:8.
[54] Revelation 13:4.
[55] Exodus 8:10; 15:11; Deuteronomy 3:24; Isaiah 40:18, 25; 44:7; 46:5; Psalms 35:10; 71:19; 86:8; 89:8; 113:5; Micah 7:18.
[56] Daniel 7:8, 25; Revelation 13:5.
[57] Revelation 13:6.
[58] 2 Thessalonians 2:4.
[59] Revelation 17:1.
[60] Jeremiah 51:13; Psalms 137.
[61] Jeremiah 3:6-10.
[62] Ezek 26-28; Isaiah 23:8, 15-18; Nahum 3:4.
[63] Isaiah 29:9; Hosea 4:11-12.
[64] Revelation 17:3.
[65] Revelation 17:4.

[66] Jeremiah 4:30.
[67] Revelation 17:5-6.
[68] Daniel 4:30.
[69] Daniel 5:30-31.
[70] Revelation 17:6.
[71] Revelation 13:16-17.
[72] Revelation 17:16.
[73] Zechariah 5:11.
[74] Revelation 17:10.
[75] Revelation 17:11.

CHAPTER 11

THE ROMAN CATHOLIC CHURCH AND THE WOMAN RIDING THE BEAST

There is an important digression we must make at this point, or else a notable and potentially harmful theory is left unaddressed. We previously identified the woman riding the beast in Revelation 17 as both the spirit of Babylon and the city of Babylon – both of which have a dreadful future destiny. There are countless other candidates that have been put forward over the years which attempt to explain the mystery of the harlot, but each conjecture has inconsistencies and many face insurmountable challenges. However, the identification of the harlot woman as the Roman Catholic Church is a common and popular view within Protestant Christianity. It is important that we treat this identification objectively and draw accurate conclusions because, as it will become clear in the next section, the Roman Catholic Church played an integral role in the subsequent 'revivals' of the 'Roman Empire'.

It is difficult to pinpoint the exact origin of this identification, but certainly just prior to the Reformation in the sixteenth century we have evidence that reformers popularised the view through sermons and written tracts. Of greater importance to us though are the reasons that lie at the foundation of this identification. Reformers clearly saw the Roman Catholic Church as a visible counterpart to the scarlet woman in Revelation 17, and as such found a biblical justification for their opposition to the papacy in Rome. We will consider some of the most common arguments in defence of this view.

The angel informed John that the woman riding the beast was called the 'mother of prostitutes', which could also serve as a descriptive title for the developing church in Rome.[76] Due to the ruling on clerical celibacy, which was formalised at the Council of Elvira in 305, sexual sin became rampant within the ecclesiastical structures of Rome. Marozia, the favoured mistress of Pope Sergius III (904-911) gave birth to Johannes who later became Pope John XI (931-935). Just twenty years later, Pope John XII turned the Lateran Palace into a brothel and had his own personal harem of concubines. Prostitutes flooded into Rome to satisfy the needs of the clergy – the offspring of whom rose to positions of power and control. Rampant fornication spread throughout the priesthood in Europe. Whilst visiting Germany, St. Boniface wrote a damning report to Pope Zachary (741-752): 'Young men who spent their youth in rape and adultery were rising in the ranks of the clergy. They were spending their nights in bed with four or five women, then getting up in the morning…to celebrate mass.'[77] By the late Middle Ages the situation of illegitimate children in Rome was so great that Pope Pius II exclaimed that Rome 'was the only city run by bastards'!'[78]

Not only could reformers find adequate evidence of the Roman Catholic Church fulfilling the nature and characteristics of the woman straddling the Roman Empire, they also saw clear parallels between her outward attire that John recorded and that of the emerging priesthood in Rome. As we have noted, John saw that the woman was dressed in purple and scarlet material that was adorned with precious stones. In her hand was a golden cup containing 'abominable things'.[79] The priesthood adopted the aforementioned colours for their liturgical robes and also prescribed that a lavish cup should be used for communion. Broderick's edition of The Catholic Encyclopedia states: '[It is] the most important of the sacred vessels…[It] may be of gold or silver, if the latter, then the inside must be surfaced with gold.'[80]

It was arguably the use of this cup, said to contain the redemptive blood of the Messiah, to achieve economic dominion over Europe that provided the fuel for the Reformation. The financial crisis within the Roman Catholic Church began when Pope Clement V shared the wealth of the church treasury amongst his relatives. His successor, Pope John XXII (1316-1334), inherited the ensuing fiscal chaos. The pope developed a new doctrine that solved the problem and once again saw inordinate wealth and lands pour into the church coffers: selling absolution from sin. Pope John XXII literally devised a list detailing the price that would need to be paid for committing various sins! In essence, the more grievous the sin, the higher the price that the perpetrator would have to pay in order to access the cup of forgiveness. The doctrine was not only expediently used by the church to tax the laity, but also by sections of the nobility to lead lives of unbridled sensuality.

By the early sixteenth century, the Dominican friar and preacher Johann Tetzel became famous for selling indulgences for those who had already died and were in purgatory. He became known for the saying: 'As soon as a coin in the coffer rings - the soul from purgatory springs'. It was the friar's flagrant abuse of his clerical position and misuse of the word of God that prompted Martin Luther to write his Ninety-Five Theses, which in turn sparked the Reformation.

The similarities between the woman of Revelation 17 and the Roman Catholic Church went even further. The woman in John's vision was 'drunk with the blood of the saints, the blood of those who bore testimony to Jesus.'[81] Undoubtedly for non-Catholic Christians living in Europe, the Roman Catholic Church was their most aggressive persecutor during the Middle Ages. In 1184, Pope Lucius III created the Papal Inquisition through the bull *Ad Abolendam*, in order to combat the Albigensian heresy in Southern France. Tribunals of the Papal Inquisition were set up throughout Europe to purge the Holy Roman Empire of heresy and had considerable power to arrest, torture and sentence those found guilty. In his historical publication,

The burning of a 16th-century Dutch Anabaptist Anneken Hendriks, who was charged with heresy.

Canon Llorente estimated that by the early nineteenth century the Papal Inquisition in Spain had condemned three million people, of whom around three hundred thousand were burned at the stake for not recanting and converting to Catholicism.

For the reformers at the time of the Reformation in the early sixteenth century, the Roman Catholic Church was none other than the woman riding the beast in Revelation 17. Certainly, the woman sitting on the seven hills was a clear reference to Rome – where the chair of St. Peter was, and still is, situated. However, one of the most fateful objections to this view is the clear reference to the literal city of Babylon found in Revelation chapters 17 and 18. It was perhaps the work of the Scottish minister Alexander Hislop in relation to this objection that has paved the way for others to continue the reformers' view to this very day.

In 1853 Hislop wrote a highly provocative pamphlet entitled *Two Babylons*. Five years later the pamphlet was significantly expanded, and in 1919 it was published as a book: *The Two Babylons or The Papal Worship Proved to be the Worship of Nimrod and His Wife*. Although more recent archaeological discoveries have served to prove that his work has numerous inaccuracies, Hislop provided a convincing connection between the ancient Babylonian pagan religion introduced by Nimrod and Semiramis, and that of the emerging brand of Christianity found in Rome. As his title makes clear, Hislop concludes that Roman Catholicism is a continuation of ancient Babylonian paganism. At the end of the nineteenth century, Hislop had given fresh life to the traditional view held by the Protestant reformers. Proponents of this view could show how the religion of Babylon had moved to Rome, and in turn, had entered the church there. The Roman Catholic Church can then be viewed as an entity that had quite literally dominated the successive European empires. Any scriptural references to a future judgement of Babylon could be satisfied by stating that the Roman Catholic Church had replaced Babylon.

Arguably the late popular dispensationalist author Dave Hunt produced the most clear and well-researched treatise on this view in his book *A Woman Rides the Beast – The Roman Catholic Church and the Last Days*, first published in 1994. Not only does Hunt develop the idea that the Roman Catholic Church straddles a 'revived Roman

Empire', he argues that the church's current pursuit of ecumenicalism is an attempt to unite all faiths in anticipation of the antichrist. Having sold approximately four million books in over forty different languages, Hunt's book *A Woman Rides the Beast* serves to demonstrate how popular this view still is today.

Although we have made a different conclusion to that of Hunt, Hislop and the reformers before them, a satisfactory explanation needs to be given to explain why the Roman Catholic Church, particularly at the height of its moral collapse in the sixteenth century, was comparable to the woman riding the beast that John recorded in Revelation 17. The answer is more fully understood in our next chapter, but simply put: the spirit of Babylon influenced the infant church in Rome. The fruit of this influence has already been noted, but Protestant Christianity has often failed to note how the Roman Catholic Church has, for the most part, freed itself from this influence and has entered into a season of renewal.

Pope John XXIII published a prayer that was to be said daily throughout the world during Vatican II Council (1962-1965), which asked the Holy Spirit to 'renew your wonders in this, our day, as a new Pentecost'. Clearly Vatican II marked a pursuit of the Holy Spirit – a pursuit that was answered in dramatic fashion during the 'Duquesne weekend'. In 1967 a group of Catholic students from Duquesne University went on retreat to study the Acts of the Apostles and the claims made by Pentecostals about modern-day baptism in the Holy Spirit. One night the students received their own Pentecost; they were filled with the Holy Spirit and began to speak in tongues. Due to the openness to the Holy Spirit provided by Vatican II, and the endorsement of the Charismatic Renewal by Pope John XXIII and his successors Pope Paul VI and Pope John Paul II, the outpouring of the Holy Spirit spread across the Roman Catholic Church. To date, it is estimated that seventy-two million Catholics have been touched by the Charismatic Renewal, been baptised in the Holy Spirit and speak in tongues. The Charismatic Renewal stands as a sign to Protestants that God has not rejected any aspects or branches of the Christian Church, but is rather drawing all together by and through the Holy Spirit – so that many streams may eventually form one river.

So, as we rejoin the historical narrative of our journey at the collapse of the Western Roman Empire, and consider the influence the spirit of Babylon had on the infant church in Rome, it will be important to remember this recent and most provocative symbol of God's grace. Despite its morbid past, there awaits a glorious future for the Roman Catholic Church.

---

[76] Revelation 17:5.
[77] Hunt, Dave, *A Woman Rides the Beast*, Eugene, Origen: Harvest House Publishers, 1994, p165.
[78] *Ibid.*, p.164.
[79] Revelation 17:4.
[80] Hunt, *Beast,* p.74.
[81] Revelation 17:6.

CHAPTER 12

THE STORY SO FAR

In this first section, the character and essence of the Roman Empire have been set out to show a relevant connection with Nebuchadnezzar's dream in Daniel chapter 2 and the visions of Daniel in chapter 7. A case has also been made for an extension of the fourth kingdom in some form (albeit a mixture of iron and clay) until the arrival of a fifth and enduring kingdom established at the appearing of the Son of Man. A survey of the history following the collapse of the Roman Empire in the West will provide us with startling evidence to demonstrate how this empire, unlike any other in history, has been 'revived' time and again in Europe, fitting the description of the feet of the statue.

As we now journey into the second section, the essential 'Roman' characteristics will be used to compare and contrast 'revivals' of the 'Roman Empire' in European history. We have already noted that in the case of Europe, the Roman Empire failed due to its inability to rule over the Frankish geographical area. Recurring patterns of this failing to rule Europe as a whole will therefore be of particular interest to us. However, if we are looking at an empire that is in essence 'Roman', or a prophetic fulfilment as Irenaeus anticipated, there are limits to which a comparison with the ancient Roman Empire can be made. Therefore, defining a subsequent 'empire' as a 'revived Roman Empire' has to be weighed in the light of the evidence presented. In the section that follows, evidence will be evaluated for seven distinct episodes of European history that can be viewed as 'revivals' of the 'Roman Empire'.

CHAPTER 13

LIFE BEYOND THE GRAVE!

Despite the demise of the Roman Empire in Europe, both the strength and dream of Rome was inherited and continued by the Catholic Church. On 28 October 312, Emperor Constantine fought against Maxentius in the famous Battle of Milvian Bridge. The Emperor's religious affairs adviser, Lactantius, recounts that Constantine and his soldiers had a vision of the Christian God promising victory if they daubed the sign of the cross on their shields. Although we cannot verify the exact details of what took place, legend has it that Constantine's soldiers obeyed the vision and overcame their enemies. Aside from the religious significance of a pagan army using a Christian symbol, the battle was also fused with political significance. Constantine's victory ended the Tetrarchy, introduced by Diocletian in 293, making him the sole ruler of the Roman Empire.

Following this historic victory and shift in the political administration of the empire, Emperor Constantine legalised Christianity under the Edict of Milan in February 313. This allowed individuals to follow the faith of their choosing, and so granted Christians protection from persecution. The property of Christians and churches that had previously been confiscated was returned. Due to the severity of their previous persecution, the edict literally meant life rather than death for the growing Christian population in the Roman Empire. Clearly, Constantine was paying homage to the Christian God who granted him success over the empire.

Despite Constantine's personal profession of faith in God and the construction of many impressive Christian buildings, such as the

Church of the Holy Sepulchre and Old St. Peter's Basilica, Constantine maintained a devotion to pagan practices. The clearest reference to this is the Arch of Constantine, erected to commemorate his victory against Maxentius. This was decorated with images of the goddess Victoria and sacrifices to gods such as Apollo, Diana, and Hercules, but contained no Christian symbolism. In 321, Constantine instructed that Christians and non-Christians should be united in observing the venerable day of the sun, referencing the esoteric Eastern sun worship which Aurelian had introduced, and whose coinage still carried the symbols of the sun cult until 324.

The Arch of Constantine in Rome

This fusion of pagan and Christian faith practiced by Constantine reflected the essence of what the Roman Empire had become. Rome had previously founded its religion and politics on paganism, with Church Father Jerome calling her 'the sink of all superstitions'.[82] Long before the birth of the Church, Rome had already become a spiritual empire, in which citizens were encouraged to honour the cult of Rome. When the Roman Empire elected Christianity as its religion, the infant church in Rome became the state church. In such a union compromises had to be made: both popular paganism and the cult of Rome flooded into the church. As a result, the Catholic Church[2] reflected the fusion of the Christian and pagan practices that were present in Emperor Constantine.

---

2   Historians use numerous titles to refer to the church led by the papacy in Rome. After the First Council of Nicaea in 325, generally speaking, the title Catholic Church is used. However by 1045 the Greek-speaking church of the Eastern Roman Empire separated from the Catholic Church in Rome. The former became the Orthodox Church and the latter the Roman Catholic Church. When we need to refer to the governance of the Roman Catholic Church by the pope in the city of Rome, we will use an additional title: The Holy See.

This helps historians understand how quickly paganism, the essence of Roman belief, disappeared from Rome after its official prohibition in 381. The speed with which official paganism disappeared from Rome is incomparable to that of any other ancient or popular superstition in history. The renowned Roman historian Edward Gibbon traces the 'ruin of paganism' from this historic point, by referencing how key components of the old religious and political system in Rome were absorbed and rebranded through the state church. Perhaps the most identifiable of the pagan events that was christianised was that of the chief imperial cult of *Sol Invictus*, the Unconquered Sun, whose main temple was dedicated on 25 December. This became Christmas, the celebration of the birth of Jesus Christ! In 395, the bishop of Rome affirmed the ascendancy he assumed over other Bishops by taking the pagan title of *Pontifex*, from which the currently used word 'pope' derives. This precedent set in Rome enabled Christianity, through the Catholic Church and missionaries, to spread west across Europe, with occupied peoples being able to continue their pagan rituals under Christian names and guises.

More importantly, the Catholic Church became a part of the Roman Empire, carrying its identity and essence, pushing other expressions of Christianity, such as Celtic Christianity, to the margins. The Roman brand of Christianity was declared as the state religion of the empire in 380. Constantine's biographer and theologian, Eusebius, argued that the empire was the vehicle through which Christianity would spread to the world. Constantine and other Christians at the time must have viewed this monumental transition from paganism to Christianity as confirmation that a new spiritual empire was being born, one in which the motivation and reasons for conquest took on a new religious perspective.

Constantine's defeat of rival Emperor Licinius in the great civil war of 324, caused by Licinius reneging on the promises made in the Edict of Milan and persecuting Christians, came to represent the defeat of a rival centre of pagan and Greek-speaking political activity in the Eastern Empire. It was therefore proposed that a new eastern capital should represent the integration of the East into the Roman Empire as a whole, as a centre of learning, prosperity, and cultural preservation for the whole of the Eastern Roman Empire. Constantine rebuilt Byzantium and renamed it Constantinople.

The Christianisation of the Roman Empire led to the 'imperialisation' of Roman Christianity. The relocation of the emperor to the eastern capital left the bishops of Rome as defenders, not only of the traditions of the apostles, but also of the classical thinkers and governments. As a result, Roman Christianity, already demonstrated as a mixture of Christianity and paganism, was to have yet a third influence from the philosophers and politicians. This resulted in the state church of the Roman Empire carrying a conviction that it represented a superior and advanced culture. When the Catholic Church considered mission, it viewed success as a country adopting, in its entirety, this new culture and way of life.

By the beginning of the fifth century, the Roman Empire in the West was in crisis. Although the causes of its collapse are both numerous and complex, the fall of the Western Roman Empire was precipitated by the invasion of barbarian tribes: the Visigoths, Vandals and Huns. Interestingly, the Germans who settled on Roman land tended to abandon tribal gods in favour of the unique brand of Christianity that had been left behind. In the following two centuries a Romanised form of Germanic society emerged in the West.

The European converts to Christianity naturally looked to the priests of their new faith for guidance, causing the papacy in Rome to grow in power and influence over the various tribes and peoples that now fought openly in the geopolitical space the old Roman Empire had left behind. Although the western side of the empire was shattered, the papacy gave it a unique continuity due to the Catholic Church containing much of the essence of what was Roman. The English Philosopher Thomas Hobbes records: 'The papacy is none other than the ghost of the deceased Roman Empire, sitting crowned upon the grave thereof.'[83] The Roman Legions may have failed to uphold the Roman Empire in Europe, but the state church of the empire had succeeded.

The Franks were the first of the Germanic peoples to fill the vacuum. Clovis, king of the Franks, defeated the last Gallo-Roman ruler at the Battle of Soissons in 486 and established the Merovingian monarchy. With this victory, the remaining elements of the imperial government fell into his hands, namely the fiscal lands, coinage, the tax administration and, perhaps most importantly, the remainder of the army including its arms factories.

Ten years later, Clovis converted to the aforementioned Roman Christianity that had evolved in Europe. As a result, Clovis was hailed as a new Constantine. He not only continued the Caesars' religion, but also the rich Roman heritage that was left behind. Although the Roman Empire in the West had been defeated and was passing into antiquity, it was given immediate life and continuance through the Franks. This Frankish empire united various Germanic tribes including the Alemanni, Saxons and Bavarians. It was generally Christian, with influence from both Roman and Celtic missionaries, with monasteries and churches built and maintained by their nobility.

The success of Clovis in doing this was recognised by the Eastern Roman Emperor Anastasius in 508, when he granted Clovis an honorary consulship and transmitted to him the insignia of the royal office: a purple tunic, a cloak and a diadem. It was this recognition from the seat of the emperor in Constantinople that placed Clovis, and subsequent Merovingian rulers, in an imperial context.

After Clovis' death in 511, his kingdom passed through his line for over two hundred years. Not one of his successors abandoned Roman ways and customs, with the imperial context remaining. These kings stood as guarantors of the legal order and external peace, therefore presenting themselves as lawgivers, just as the Caesars before them had done. They continued the Roman administrative system to govern the large lands they inherited. For example, in Gaul they continued the Roman system of taxation and tolls in order to obtain large sums of money to help fund their standing army. The Merovingians central government was also organised according to a pattern provided by Rome.

With the Catholic Church forming a central part of the administration in the provinces of the Frankish territory, the appointment of bishops became a central area of debate between the monarchy and the ambition of the pontiff in Rome. The Catholic Church had been politicised by Emperor Diocletian when he established one hundred and one dioceses as units of local government. The bishops were political agents for the pope to carry out church policy, holding, as they saw it, the eternal fate of men in their hands. This tension between the Merovingians and the papacy led to a fundamental disagreement between King Clothar II and Pope Gregory I. Clothar insisted that the clergy were his servants first and foremost, and Gregory failed to persuade him otherwise. The much needed support by the Catholic Church from the Merovingian monarchs then ceased. Gregory I died in 604 and the Holy See fell into internal crisis. For the next two centuries there were thirty-two popes, with twenty-three in office for less than five years. On two occasions rival popes and antipopes contended the chair of St. Peter!

Aside from the bloodshed and infighting, the popes were preoccupied with Byzantine over-lordship and the threat from the Lombards of Northern Italy. The scene was now set for the next critical development of the continuation of the Roman Empire: the rise of Charlemagne.

---

[82] Alexander Hislop, The Two Babylon's or The Papal worship proved to be the worship of Nimrod and his wife, Popular Edition, Topeka, Kansas: S.W Partridge & CO., 1952, p.250.

[83] Hunt, *Beast*, p95.

CHAPTER 14

CHARLEMAGNE

The future of Europe was about to change. One man and his family would seek to alter the balance of power in Francia, present day France and Germany, arguably the centre of western Europe. Pepin the Short, father of Charlemagne, planned to overthrow King Childeric III and in doing so the reign of the Merovingians over the Frankish chieftains. However, due to the Roman Christianity that was being formalised in Frankish territory and the population's growing loyalty to the Catholic Church, Pepin concluded that legitimacy for such a coup could only be granted by one individual - Pope Zacharias.

Bust of Charlemagne, in Aachen, Germany

Due to the chaos in the Holy See and the imminent danger from the Lombards, Pope Zacharias saw the benefit of a new powerful ally, one through whom he could reassert his control over the clergy and the power of the Catholic Church in Europe. In 751, Pope Zacharias sent Boniface, Archbishop of Mainz, to crown Pepin and his two sons, Charlemagne and Carloman, as king of the Franks. The coronation took place in 752. The politically and militarily motivated appointment of

Pepin worked; in the minds of the religious population the new regime had been divinely appointed – God had elected Pepin and his family as royalty. The wider significance of the papacy being involved in the coronation of the king of Francia will be discussed later.

The pope quite literally forced Childeric III into monastic living by having his head shaved, dressing him in sackcloth and confining him to the monastery at Saint-Bertin. Clearly, the Merovingian dynasty was humiliated and finished. At this point, the Roman and Frankish regimes became intimately connected and interdependent; they would either stand or fall together. As a result, the spirit of the 'Roman Empire', bound in the Catholic Church, was about to be passed into the new emerging empire in the West.

In 751, the Lombards under King Aistulf defeated the troops of the Exarch of Ravenna, entered Italy and ended Byzantine rule there. After a failure to secure help from Constantinople, Pope Stephen II travelled to Frankish territories to seek help from the loyal son of the Catholic Church, Pepin the Short.

Their meeting took place at the Abbey of Saint-Denis near Paris in January 754. It was this meeting that not only sought to define the relationship between Francia and the Catholic Church, but the relationship between future emperors and popes, and with it, the balance of secular and spiritual power in Western Christendom.

The meeting became one of a salesperson seeking to entice an unwilling customer to purchase a product at a monumental cost! The pope initially tried to convince Pepin the Short of his God-given duty to support the Catholic Church against the Lombards – especially in the light of the help he had received from Pope Zacharias. Realising the tactic had failed, Pope Stephen II resorted to flattery. He sought to bamboozle the barbarian king with the idea that the Franks were linked by ancestry to the Royal House of Troy. He suggested that, just as God called the Old Testament King David, so God was now calling the Franks to become a new Israel who would set God's people free. In the words of Edward Gibbon:

The royal unction of the kings of Israel was dextrously applied: the successor of St Peter assumed the character of a divine ambassador: a German chieftain was transformed into the Lord's anointed.[84]

However, it was the use of the Donation of Constantine that would prove successful in securing Pepin's support. Although we now understand that the Donation of Constantine was a fraudulent document, it carried a convincing explanatory story which Pope Stephen II would surely have emphasised! Emperor Constantine was suffering from leprosy and travelled to Pope Sylvester I to receive baptism before his death. However, during his baptism he was miraculously healed. In return, he bequeathed to the pope not only the lands now ruled by the Lombards, but also some of his own authority as Roman Emperor:

We decree that the sacred See of Blessed Peter shall be gloriously exalted even above our Empire and earthly throne... as over all churches of God in all the world... We convey to Sylvester, universal Pope, both our palace and likewise all provinces and palaces and districts of the city of Rome and Italy and of the regions of the west.[85]

This proved enough; Pepin was convinced of his 'duty' and set out to make war on the Lombards and liberate Italy from their control.

Even more significantly, the mission of Pope Gregory I to Christianise the West was now, through the acceptance of the Donation of Constantine, the main motivating factor for both the papacy and the emperor. The spirit of the 'Roman Empire', long harboured by the state church in Rome, was now going to be spread throughout the West by both the Catholic Church and the king. We now have the first possibility of a 'revived Roman Empire' that we can compare and contrast with that which is anticipated in the Book of Daniel.

After the death of his co-heir, brother and opponent, Carloman, on 4 December 771, Charlemagne set out to do what no other Frankish king had done before him - bring peace to the three-way power struggle that existed between Francia, Lombardy and the papacy in Italy. Charlemagne held Desiderius, king of the Lombards, under siege in Pavia. Desiderius sued for peace in the summer of 774 and Charlemagne took the 'Iron Crown' of Lombardy and set himself up as the king of both the Franks and the Lombards.

By the age of thirty-seven, Charlemagne had established himself as the ruler of the Christian West, one in which a new Francia emerged: a fusion of Frankish custom, Celtic spirituality and Romano-papal ecclesiastical politics. In this new design, the papacy saw itself as the guiding father to this new elite class that would descend from Charlemagne. Meanwhile Charlemagne developed the doctrine of 'Two Swords' as a means by which he could implement his own personal mission. In one hand he held a sword over the empire, which he was to advance as God's ambassador. In the other hand, he held a sword over the clergy and the Catholic Church, which he must protect and maintain.

For Charlemagne, the 'revived Roman Empire' in the West needed to separate itself from the failing eastern capital in Constantinople. In 794 he called the first western Church council in Frankfurt, clearly differentiating the authority and autonomy of the Catholic Church from the fractured Greek-speaking church of the East. He created a new capital in Aachen, Westphalia, where he built his royal residence. By the turn of the century, the Western Empire had its own capital and independent church led by the pope in Rome.

The process of deliberate separation from the east of the empire was furthered by Charlemagne's development of diplomatic relations with those previously aligned only to Constantinople. First the Levantine ruler and Islamic emperor, Sultan Harun al-Raschid, refused to speak with Irene, the first female emperor of the Eastern Roman Empire, viewing her as an imposter. Instead he dealt with Charlemagne whom he now regarded as the true spokesperson of Christian Europe. Furthermore, Charlemagne then received delegations from the Patriarch of Jerusalem - effectively implying that the leader of the church there now saw Charlemagne and his 'European empire' as the protector of the sacred sites. It was as if the political and spiritual role of the emperor in the East had shifted to king of the Franks in the West, making Charlemagne, rather than Irene, the true successor of the Caesars.

When Pope Hadrian I died in 795, Charlemagne engraved onto his tomb: 'Hadrian and Charles, I a King, you a Father.' With the spiritual 'Roman Empire' being fostered in the Catholic Church, and extended

The Final World Empire

through its guidance of the kings of the growing Frankish kingdom, it was clear that the unique relationship, perhaps originally intended by Pope Stephen II, was now complete. However, a king is not an emperor, and an emperor was needed for the Catholic Church's ambition to be fulfilled, if this new fusion is to be correctly termed a 'revival' of the ancient Roman Empire.

This is precisely what happened. After Hadrian's death, Pope Leo III was elected, and due to his lack of lineage to the city's leading elite families, Rome divided into factions warring over his legitimacy to lead the Catholic Church. The pope's position became even more untenable when his personal life was exposed as one of a fornicator and perjurer. In April 799, during the Saints Day procession, Leo was ambushed and brutally attacked by a band of henchman armed with knives. The men attempted to skewer Leo, but failed, leaving the pope to recover from his wounds.

Charlemagne, seeing once again the chair of St. Peter in disarray, carried out his role of defender of the Catholic Church by escorting Pope Leo III back to Rome and dealing decisively with Leo's accusers. Leo was not slow to reward the king for restoring him as head of the Holy See – a reward that would alter the future of Europe for the subsequent millennium.

In 800 the king and pope met together in the Lateran Palace. There, in the main audience chamber, stood a mosaic symbolising the transition that was about to take place in the policy of *revovaito Romanorum imperii*, 'reviving the Roman Empire'! In the mosaic, St. Peter stood handing a stole of office to Pope Leo and a battle standard to Charlemagne. It was plain for the audience to see that the Catholic Church, as the inheritor and defender of the cultures, customs and religion of Rome, was portrayed as divinely appointed alongside Charlemagne, who was to advance this 'revived kingdom' by force in the name of God. It was in front of this mosaic that Leo clothed Charlemagne in purple and received from him the keys to the sacred sites of Jerusalem – ending the eastern emperors' rights over the city.

On Christmas Day, Pope Leo III acquired a role that once belonged to that of the Pagan College of Pontiffs in Rome, the ability to crown the emperor. Once he placed the crown on Charlemagne's head he said:

'Long life and victory to Charlemagne, the most pious Augustus, the great, the peace loving emperor, crowned by God.'[86]

The process of separation between East and West was now complete. In the West there now stood a new Latinised empire ruled by an emperor, with its own capital and its own church, a complete contradistinction to the Roman Empire in the East. Through the history of loyalties to ancient Rome, both the Catholic Church and Europe stood as decidedly more 'Roman' in nature than the Greek-speaking Eastern Empire.

The crowning of Charlemagne changed the future of Europe, as Gibbon writes: 'Europe dates a new era from his restoration of the Western Empire'.[87] The development of Europe was now destined to be one of an urbanised Christianity, which would see the advancement of the thinking and ambition of a 'Roman Empire' that the European people had once defeated. Pope Benedict XVI in his book *Europe Today and Tomorrow* writes:

> *Independently of this history of the term Europe, the establishment of the kingdom of the Franks, as the Roman Empire that had declined and was now reborn, signifies, indeed, a decisive step toward what we mean today when we speak of Europe.*[88]

The significance of the crowning of Charlemagne cannot be overestimated in its importance to the development of both the Catholic Church and Europe. However, Charlemagne's compliance in the process is somewhat questionable. His relationship with the pope was not subservient, and although Charlemagne was called 'Caesar', and the inheritor of Augustus, he refused to use the title. It is also unlikely that Charlemagne viewed his appointment as a resurrection of the 'Roman Empire.' Such a romantic notion would not have appealed to either the Franks or the Catholic Church at the turn of the ninth century, because both viewed the classical heritage of the Roman Empire with distrust.

For the Franks, there was a level of pride carried in defeating the Roman armies led by Publius Quinctilius Varus in 9 AD in the famous battle in the Teutoborg Forest in Germania. This saw a halt to Roman expansion, and ultimately preserved the Frankish territories from being

Romanised. Whilst for the Catholic Church, the history of the martyrs 'whom the Romans killed by sword, wild animals or fire', as Pippin III described it, was a painful memory of pagan Rome. Charlemagne had to balance carefully this new title and the Frankish leadership who may have become alienated should he turn his attention to issues in the Eastern Roman Empire.

As Charlemagne united this new empire, his chief motivation was its Christianisation. Despite his personal departure from Roman practices, they were very much carried on through the Catholic Church. Charlemagne was faced with the same problem that the Romans had before him, how to unite and keep united this diverse mass of peoples. Charlemagne soon discovered it would be the church that would enable him to do this as it provided him a secretariat, intelligentsia, senior administrators and guardians of the ethical code that could unite the empire.

However, in order to pay for this service from the Catholic Church, Charlemagne was complicit in the aggrandisement of churchmen, such as Alcuin who became the abbot of seven monasteries. Ecclesiastical titles and land were given for the pledge of allegiance from the clergy, and rulers of ecclesiastical estates were exempted from interference by imperial agents and responsible directly to the emperor.

Although Charlemagne failed to inaugurate a lasting European state, his reign is significant to us for three reasons. First, his reliance on the Catholic Church to administer and provide the unity his empire required elevated various church offices to ones of great political and secular power. This in turn paved the way for the Church in the High Middle Ages to rival the power of the state by controlling the appointment to these offices and populating them with men loyal first to the pope. As we look at the development of the Catholic Church during this period, it would seem that the crowning of Charlemagne by Pope Leo III, was in fact a shrewd coup, which would be enjoyed by his successors at the expense of Charlemagne's.

Second, Charlemagne provided subsequent rulers in Europe both a challenge and a dream of a united Christian state. Europe was now a family, and all subsequent wars and factions would take place within the family as different dynasties and nations vied with each other to carry his mantle, and in doing so, provide a continuance of the 'Roman Empire' in Europe.

Third, the evidence examined concerning Charlemagne's reign and the characteristics of his empire, suggest that this empire was, in line with the primary proposition of this thesis, in fact a 'revived Roman Empire', based on the Western Roman Empire that Emperor Constantine I once ruled.

Charlemagne died in 814, leaving the empire to his son Louis. 'Louis the Pious', as he was later known, allowed the empire to fragment amongst his own three sons before his death in 840. Three years later at Verdun, an accord was reached between the brothers that split Francia into three territories: France on the west, Germany on the east and the Rhineland as a buffer between the two. The Carolingians remained as kings over these three lands until the end of the ninth century, but were pre-occupied with a threefold threat: Vikings in the north, Saracens from the south and Magyars from the east. When the Carolingian line finally failed, so too did the imperial crown once worn by Charlemagne. The resultant fracture of Francia can be compared to the failure of the Roman Empire in Europe, and the feet of iron and clay in the statue of Daniel chapter 2.

The geography of Francia will now occupy our focus for two reasons. First, Francia was the place where the Romans failed to control and dominate Europe, which can be viewed as being comparable with the condition of the feet of the statue in Daniel chapter 2. Second, Francia was the place where the first 'revival' of the 'Roman Empire' under Charlemagne and the Catholic Church took place. In the wake of its fracture after the death of Charlemagne, both France and Germany emerge as countries seeking to unite this territory until the present day. Although we will discover that other nations have attempted to identify themselves with the Roman Empire, none are able to parallel the pursuit of France and Germany in this regard.

---

[84] Edward Gibbon, *Decline and Fall of the Roman Empire*, Vol. VI, New York: Penguin USA, 1983, p.1168.

[85] Wilson, Derek, *Charlemagne, Barbarian and Emperor*, Surrey: Pimlico, 2006, p.23.
[86] Ibid., p.82.
[87] Gibbon, *Decline*, p.184.
[88] Joseph Ratzinger, *Europe Today and Tomorrow, Addressing the Fundamental Issues*, Second Edition, San Francisco: Ignatius Press, 2005, p.14.

CHAPTER 15

THE HOLY ROMAN EMPIRE

Only a century after the demise of the 'revived Roman Empire' that Charlemagne helped create, history was about to repeat itself. Once again the Holy See had fallen into crisis. Externally, the Catholic Church was at war against the Lombards, whilst internally, and perhaps more importantly, the conduct and lifestyle of Pope John XII had brought the Catholic Church into disrepute. Although it would deserve a book dedicated to a study of the pontiff's character to paint a clear and fair picture of the man, Catholics and non-Catholics alike freely point out that John lived a life of unbridled sensuality! The pope had countless sexual partners, including his own niece and the widows of fallen friends. This dangerous and somewhat perverse behaviour was not kept separate from his clerical role; rather, John welcomed sexual immorality into the church by turning the Lateran Palace into a brothel. However, perhaps of more concern to a deeply religious and spiritual society, were the frequent references to John having private communion services with the devil!

The aristocracy had seen enough. War began to break out around the chair of St. Peter. In 961, fearing for his own life, Pope John XII looked to the newly crowned king of the German nation, Otto I, for help against his accusers. Just as his Frankish antecedent Charlemagne had done, Otto crossed the Alps to rescue both the pope and the Catholic Church. Otto I succeeded in securing John's position as the pope, but on leaving Rome, John sided with the enemies of the German king. This ill-informed manoeuvre saw Otto replace John with a German nominee, with a view to bringing much-needed reform to the Catholic Church. However, Otto could not stay in Rome to ensure his nominee would succeed in being selected as pontiff, and so the following thirty-six years saw ten popes and anti-popes fight over their legitimacy to sit in the chair of St. Peter.

It was arguably this level of interference in ecclesiastical affairs at the heart of the Catholic Church that ultimately led to the conception of the Holy Roman Empire. Just as Charlemagne had done before him, Otto fused both the role of the emperor and his country, Germany, to the Catholic Church, believing that the emperor must not only protect, but must actively help bring ecclesiastical reform. Through his dynasty Germany would for years to come be the country from which the emperor would be appointed.

Only two generations later, Otto's grandson, Otto III, built upon the notion of a Holy Roman Empire – believing that such an empire would be led by the German nation. As we have previously discovered, the pope was needed to appoint the emperor, and if Otto III were to proclaim that the Holy Roman Empire had been born, the religiously devout European peoples would look to Rome for confirmation that this was of divine origin. To ensure such an outcome would be the case, a political trade-off was arranged. Otto appointed the first German pope, Gregory V, on 3 May 996, who in turn crowned Otto as Holy Roman Emperor nearly three weeks later!

Clearly the Holy Roman Empire, conceived by Otto I and established by his grandson, was a 'revival' of the 'Roman Empire.' To such ends, Otto III sought to identify the reborn empire with all things Roman. Although subsequent German emperors would have Aachen as a city reminding them of their predecessor Charlemagne and his divine mission to extend God's kingdom throughout the earth, Otto also adopted Rome as his new capital. Furthermore, in what can be seen as an attempt to identify with the Caesars from antiquity, he wore a toga and made it his official imperial dress.

The significance of these events at the end of the first

The coronation of Otto III

millennium is of paramount importance to our study. As has been shown, the practices and identity of the Roman Empire in the West was not lost at its fall in the fifth century, rather they were continued by the barbarian tribes up to the time of Charlemagne, who united the continent of Europe and received the title Caesar. In addition, the Catholic Church had fostered the spirit of the Roman Empire. At this point in history, both the Catholic Church and the empire in Europe were fused into one unit: Christendom.

Today, we often differentiate between the affairs of church and those of state, but to this emerging continent and church, there was no differentiation; it was now the Holy Roman Empire. In this empire, the pope was the supreme pontiff and the emperor the supreme ruler. The 'Roman Empire' had in fact been 'revived' and was now functional as the Holy Roman Empire, a title that would describe this fused spiritual and secular entity until the time of Napoleon in 1806.

Interestingly, in the mind of the Jewish historian Goldwurm, the Holy Roman Empire was a continuation of the Roman Empire throughout their exile from the land of Israel:

> *The powerless orphan adopted by the mighty empire, originally by Emperor Constantine I and later by his successors, grew up to utilize its unique position as state religion of the great empire and moved on to a period of unprecedented growth. Its power, whether temporal or spiritual, eclipses that of kingdoms and empires. Thus throughout our exile, the fourth kingdom is represented by the Christian church, conceived of, despite all its diverse forms, as one unit.*[89]

It would appear as if Charlemagne, through his unification of Europe, had bound the fate of both East Francia and West Francia to the never-ending pursuit of ruling a 'European Empire.' For in the same way that German monarchs followed in the traditions and legends of Charlemagne, and in doing so, united Germany to both the Catholic Church and the empire, so did France. Both France and Germany saw themselves as inheritors of the empire, and therefore struggled with each other, and the Catholic Church, for the ability to lead.

Despite the appointment of the first German pope in Gregory V by Otto III, the French soon had their nominee in the chair of St. Peter: Sylvester II, the first French pope. As France began to emerge as a nation, like Germany, they pursued ancestral links with Charlemagne. Travelling singers and poets known as *jongleurs* were popular with the people and of interest to historians, because their songs and poems provide an insight into the ambitions and desires of the nation. The most famous of such songs in France was the *Chanson Roland*, in which Charlemagne appears as Roland, who is the focal point of two themes. First, the fight between good and evil, in which God appoints Charlemagne to defend his people. Second, the stability of feudal society in France, in which Charlemagne is depicted as the defender of the Catholic Church. Therefore the *Chanson Roland* symbolises the ambition of the French people for a united Christian society, in which the king would command the support of his warriors and take them into his council.

It was the legends of Charlemagne and the ambition to continue his legacy as the rightful rulers of the empire that formed the expansionist narrative subsequent French kings followed. After Philip I, the successive three monarchies followed this narrative without wavering, and so the legacy was tightly woven into the ambitions of the Capetian dynasty. It was during this dynasty that 'The Pilgrimage of Charlemagne' was undertaken by the French royal house to Constantinople and Jerusalem, which provided some of the ambition for France's third crusade in 1190.

Just as Constantine had presented the Catholic Church with the challenges of combining state with church and paganism with Christianity, so Charlemagne left both France and Germany with an internal conflict: the challenge of uniting and expanding the empire whilst wrestling with the Catholic Church for their rightful positions in relation to it. We will discover how this tension has been ongoing right up to this very day where it currently rages at the heart of the EU. Such events will prove to be comparable with the failure of iron to mix with clay in the feet of the great statue King Nebuchadnezzar saw in Babylon so many centuries earlier.

---

[89] R. Goldwurm, quoted in Robert Anderson, *Daniel, Signs and Wonders*, Grand Rapids, Michigan: Wm. B. Eerdmans Publishing. Co., 1984, p.22.

CHAPTER 16

THE REFORMATION

The most devastating of controversies that threatened the life of the Holy Roman Empire was that of the Investiture Contest, finally settled in 1122 at the Council of Worms. As bishops held considerable political power, due to the previously discussed reforms under Diocletian, and abbots owned vast acres of land, it was of vital interest to both Rome and the emperor in their respective bids to lead the empire to have loyal servants in these ecclesiastical positions. At this stage in the struggle for temporal power, it was the Roman Catholic Church that was victorious.

During the conflict, Pope Gregory VII excommunicated German emperor Henry IV in 1076. Without the backing of Roman Catholic Church, Henry lost all legitimacy to rule. In an act of humility and repentance he walked barefoot, wearing a hair shirt, from Speyer in Germany to the Canossa Castle in January 1077 to beg the pontiff for forgiveness. The doors of the castle remained shut for three days before the humiliated emperor was invited to kneel before Gregory.

Henry IV, Holy Roman Emperor

The balance of power between the emperor and the pope had shifted in favour of the latter. This was in part due to the strategic appointment, over many years, of bishops loyal to the pope, and also the development of their own military forces. The papacy no longer needed to rely on the compliance of the Holy Roman Emperor to advance the kingdom of God by force. The papal war against the Normans in 1053 was the first such instance of the Roman Catholic Church taking up arms against its opponents with no direct help from the emperor.

By the conclusion at Worms, Emperor Henry V conceded to the papacy virtually full control over the Northern Italian Bishoprics. However, not only did the balance of power swing greatly towards the pontiff, the power of the German monarchy itself eroded. The initial excommunication of Henry IV by Pope Gregory VII had set another precedent: the king would not rule by virtue of his birthright, but rather by the acceptance of the German Princes, who had allied themselves with the pope during the contest. The role of monarch was now as *primus inter pares,* first among equals, which reinforced the fateful dualism between princes and kings in German history until the nineteenth century.

Now that the Roman Catholic Church had undergone this limited internal reformation and was somewhat free from its previous political restrictions, pontiffs took on the role that was previously ascribed to the emperor - to advance Christian civilisation throughout the world. In 1095 at the Council of Clermont, Pope Urban II declared the first Crusade to Jerusalem, to liberate the holy city from its Jewish and Muslim inhabitants. This landmark decision signifies both the continuation of the previous Roman Empire's policy of intolerance towards other religions and its foreign policy: the destruction of any civilisation that would not surrender. In Jerusalem, Jews and Muslims stood together to fight against the largely French-speaking army of knights. The walls of Jerusalem finally fell and an estimated seventy thousand Muslims and Jews were massacred. Furthermore, the religious violence returned home with the crusaders who murdered seven thousand Jews in the Rhineland in 1076, making it the first European pogrom of the Jewish people at the hands of French and German knights.

This first crusade, instigated by the papacy, set the Holy Roman Empire on a course of aggression against the Jews that can be seen as a continuance of the suffering the Jewish people endured under the Romans. As previously mentioned, the last time the Jews had to defend the walls of Jerusalem was in 70 AD against the Roman emperor Titus. Anti-Semitism in Europe is of interest to our study because the Reformation largely fractured the entity of Christendom, and yet the persecution of the Jews, as anticipated by the Church Fathers at the hands of the Roman Empire, was continued with justification from both the Catholic and Lutheran Church movements either side of the great church schism. This continuing hatred of God's people fastened itself to the emerging identity of both the German nation and the Catholic Church.

Prior to the first Crusade, the Jews living in central Europe occupied a unique position, one of middle class traders, surgeons, apothecaries, and craftsmen in gold, silver and precious stones. Since in practice, rather than in scriptural principle, the Jews had no religious prohibition on usury, they provided a money-lending service in the fiscal institutions of France and Germany, making them a very wealthy people group in both countries. The reason for this privileged and peaceful co-existence with the Barbarian tribes dwelling there was due to the fact that they reached the Rhineland and the Danube valley in the wake of the Roman Legions, long before the establishment of Christianity. They formed a literate community with an ancient heritage. The earliest written record testifying to their presence in this area is the text in a decree by Emperor Constantine in 321, preserved in the Vatican Library.

The *Judensau* at Wittenberg

The decision of Pope Urban II to take up arms against the Muslims and Jews led to centuries of Jewish suffering at the hands of German princes, and mob suspicion. Their previous position in the middle class of German society was gradually demeaned to a sub-class in which they became rag dealers, pawnbrokers, moneychangers and vagrants.

Sadly, there is evidence to support the claim that this demise in social status in Germany was a policy of the Roman Catholic Church. The church used propaganda to this end in the image of the *Judensau,* which became a common subject of Christian religious art. The image is that of a sow, under which Jewish children are drinking its milk and at its rear a Jewish Rabbi lifts its tail ready to eat its excrement. Meanwhile, Satan watches the entire scene approvingly. This image was displayed in Wittenberg in 1305 on the facade of the Stadtkirche, the church where Martin Luther preached and later nailed his Ninety-Five Theses. The vile image appeared throughout Germany and other neighbouring countries. The renditions of the *Judensau* legitimised the fears and superstitions the German people had about the Jewish people, helping perpetuate them from generation to generation.

This in turn led to a rise in anti-Semitic attacks. The most famous attack was over the myth of Simon of Trent, a young Italian boy who went missing in 1475. A group of Jewish men and women were blamed for his abduction and murder in which it was claimed they drained his body of blood to use in their Passover meal. An entire Jewish community was arrested and tortured until a spurious confession was wrested from them, after which they were burnt at the stake. This particular incident was engraved beneath a *Judensau* on a bridge tower in Frankfurt near the gateway to a Jewish ghetto, designed to act as a warning to future generations about the danger the Jewish community posed.

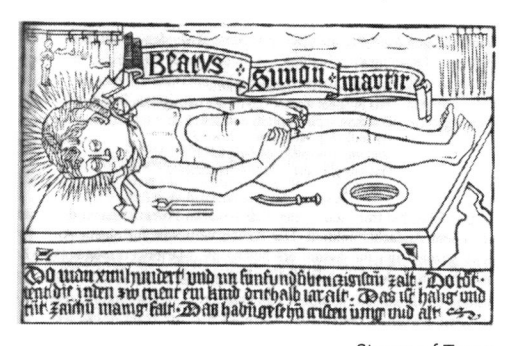

Simon of Trent

However, the anticipated persecution of the Jewish people at the hands of the fourth world empire cannot only be linked to the Roman

Catholic Church, but also to the emerging Protestant Church. Although the Reformation began due to Martin Luther's own desire to reform the Roman Catholic Church from its numerous abuses, he did not view its open persecution of the Jewish people as one of them. In fact, Luther continued German anti-Semitism when he sought to re-address the role and place of the Jewish people in God's plan of redemption. In 1543 Luther published a sixty-five thousand word treatise called 'On the Jews and their lies' in which he wrote that the Jews were 'a base, whoring people, that is, no people of God, and their boast of lineage, circumcision, and law must be accounted as filth'.[90] Furthermore, Luther went as far as to suggest how a Jewish pogrom should be carried out, and how those who initiate such acts of violence against them are free from blame and judgement. Therefore, the resultant acts of anti-Semitism in Germany and Europe during the sixteenth century cannot be blamed entirely on the Roman Catholic Church, but also upon the infant Protestant Church.

Martin Luther

The work of Martin Luther was very popular amongst the German Princes and other European monarchs, who saw his questioning of the financial ambitions of the papacy as an expedient justification to regain control of their own financial affairs and lands from the Roman Catholic Church, particularly following losses during the Investiture Contest. As a result, the Reformation spread throughout the Holy Roman Empire, and made way for other reformers, such as Ulrich Zwingli in Switzerland, and John Calvin from France, to add theological breadth and diversity to the growing movement.

Learned Protestants calling themselves *literats* produced materials in which they looked back to the original authoritative sources, *Ad fontes*, that common Catholic doctrine was said to be developed from, and ultimately rejected most of them. Their works were produced with the populace in mind and became the common discussion in salons, universities and courts throughout the remainder of the century. This upsurge of popular theology, with its emphasis on biblical authority over tradition and Christ's headship over the Church in place of the headship of the pope, undoubtedly led to the demise of Christendom as a religio-political entity. No longer was there one true church at the heart of the Holy Roman Empire but many.

Eventually, the Reformation eroded the foundations of Christendom to such a degree that the Holy Roman Empire entered war with itself in what became known as the Thirty Years' War. Although there were numerous and complex reasons for this war, which started in Germany and eventually involved most of Europe, at the centre lay the battle of religion fought between the Catholics and the Protestants. During this conflict, millions of lives were lost, commerce was destroyed, farmland was rendered unproductive and social order throughout Germany broke down. However, something of a new Europe emerged in its wake.

In 1648 the Peace of Westphalia was declared to end the suffering caused by the war. It contained the conclusion on the issue of religion for the continent to pursue. An individual citizen of a nation was to be treated equally in matters of state, regardless of whether their declared religion was the same as the king. Therefore the Peace of Westphalia hailed the demise of Christendom, for the pope was no longer the father of the pure faith who would guide the emperor on a combined mission to Christianise the world. The emperor, like all other members of the empire, was free to choose his own expression of Christianity. The interdependent relationship between the Roman Catholic Church and state, formed in the days of Charlemagne, had ended.

Although the idea of Christendom had perished as a result of the Peace of Westphalia, the basic structure of the Holy Roman Empire continued until 1806. Yet, the words of Voltaire in the following century provide an interesting insight into the changing nature of the empire: 'This agglomeration which was called and which still calls itself the Holy Roman Empire was neither holy, nor Roman, nor an empire.'[91] The diminished role of the Roman Catholic Church, which in itself contained a continuance of the ancient empire and its customs and traditions, resulted in the death of this 'revival' of the 'Roman Empire'.

In Northern Europe, the Roman Catholic Church started to lose its structure, with only sixty of its six hundred and twenty churches remaining Catholic after the Peace of Westphalia. From 1648, Europe was seen as the entity in which the people of the Holy Roman Empire would put their trust as judge of international affairs. As a result, the battles between the German Habsburgs and the French Valois and Bourbon kings intensified, as both nations wrestled to dominate and provide political leadership for the continent. Eventually the Habsburgs lost the struggle, and so power swung in favour of the French, and with it, a further 'revival' of the 'Roman Empire' took place.

---

[90] Robert Michael, *Holy Hatred: Christianity, Anti-Semitism, and the Holocaust*, New York: Palgrave Macmillan, 2006, p.111.

[91] Voltaire, "The Holy Roman Empire's Imperial Diet: Electoral Votes in 1792" *Ed. Stephen Millar, The Napoleon Series,* < http://www.napoleon-series.org/research/government/c_holyroman.html> [accessed 1 Sep 2011].

CHAPTER 17

THE FRENCH EMPIRE

Louis XIV began his personal rule as the king of France in 1661 during the Huguenot revolt. Louis, or the 'Sun King,' as he was later called, based his reign on Caesar Augustus and Charlemagne. As we shall discover, Louis saw himself as Caesar of the ancient Roman Empire in Europe and sought to follow in the footsteps of his distant predecessor Charlemagne.

In French history and folklore, Charlemagne stood as the quintessence of the French monarchy. By identifying his reign with that of Charlemagne, Louis XIV was able to assert radical control over France whilst appeasing the masses with the notion that he was simply doing that which the great Charlemagne had done. Whether the French king's motives in emulating Charlemagne's reign were romantic or expedient, Charlemagne provided a perfect example for Louis XIV to follow. The similarities between the two men are startling.

Louis XIV was an absolutist, holding power by the dominance of his character, just as Charlemagne had been. Louis frequently went to war to strengthen his borders, as Charlemagne had done. The political system Louis developed made up of *intendants,* who kept close scrutiny on the aristocracy, was similar to the royal *missi* that Charlemagne had used for the same purpose. Both men were religious and exercised control over the churches in their nation, whilst continuing in Catholic communion and obedience to the pontiff in Rome.

By understanding his predecessor's battle against paganism, Louis saw the Protestant movement of the Huguenots in France as his war of religion. The Edict of Nantes, which was introduced in 1598 by Henry IV, granted religious freedom to Protestant groups. In 1685 Louis XIV renounced the Edict of Nantes, which made Protestantism illegal. As a result, the Huguenots were faced with a dreadful future: forcible conversion or exile from France.

French propagandists promoted the idea to the French people that Louis XIV was in fact a reincarnation of Charlemagne. Gabriel David, the official historian appointed by Louis XIV, made it his primary task to glorify the monarchy and demonstrate that France was God's chosen people, whose greatest kings were Charlemagne and Louis XIV. This soon became an ideology that presented Louis XIV leading France towards a spiritual destiny, one that would provide a divine plan for humanity.

It was on this point of spiritual destiny that the Sun King and Charlemagne differed. Although Charlemagne saw divine providence on his rise to imperial greatness, he viewed it as somewhat distinct from the way the Roman Caesars saw themselves in this matter. This perhaps explains some of his reluctance to use the title 'Caesar'. Louis, however, embraced the idea that he was a continuance of the Roman Caesars. This notion was embodied in a golden statue Louis commissioned in which he was shown wearing a cuirass and sandals, seated on a bronze horse in the centre of Lyon. Like Augustus, the French king also believed that all arts, letters and sciences must come together to glorify his reign.

The identification Louis XIV sought with Charlemagne and the Caesars was not a peculiarity of his reign, rather a projection of French identity and mission that continued long after his death in 1715. By the time of the French Revolution in the latter part of the eighteenth century, France was immersed in ancient Roman ideals. Although the Revolution sought to abolish and replace the monarchy with a democratic republic, the

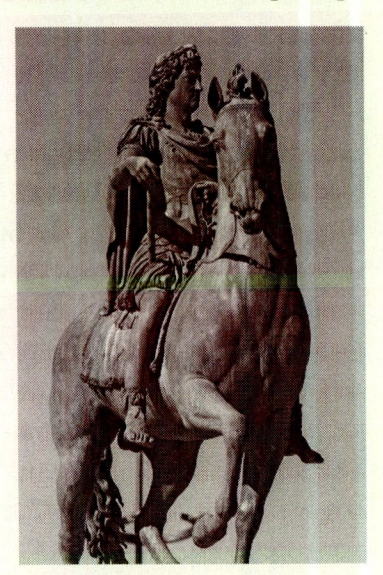

Statue of Louis XIV in Lyon, France

revolutionaries used the narrative provided by the Roman Empire expediently.

Maximilien François Marie Isidore de Robespierre, 1758 - 1794, was one of the most well-known and influential characters of the Revolution, helping to instigate the Reign of Terror. He himself became known as 'the Roman,' due to his infatuation with classical Rome. This infatuation soon took hold of the culture of France, which gradually became one that was obsessed with Rome.

Jacques-Louis David, a close friend of Robespierre, was a highly influential neoclassical painter and a dictator of the arts and culture in France during the Revolution. His famous painting of the Oath of the Horatii in 1784 demonstrates French desire for the asceticism and patriotism that was associated with the Roman Empire. The painting illustrates the three sons of Horatius swearing on their swords, held by their father, affirming that they will defend Rome to the death. The brothers battle against the Curiatii, three very different brothers who stood in opposition to Rome. Only one of the Horatii survived, and upon returning to his home in Rome, discovered his sister weeping over one of the Curiatii to whom she was secretly engaged. He then murdered his sister and was promptly arrested, but made his appeal that it was only reasonable to execute his sister because of her lack of allegiance to Rome. This story became a key cornerstone of the message of the French Revolution; feelings were to be separated from patriotism, and allegiance to the state was of paramount importance.

So on the one hand, although Louis XIV was symbolic of that which the

Oath of the Horatii, by Jacques-Louis David in 1784

Revolution stood against, the aspiration of being a continuance of the 'Roman Empire' in Europe was so deeply woven into the French nation as it emerged alongside Germany, that the concept reached its climax shortly after the Revolution with the rise of Napoleon Bonaparte.

When Napoleon prepared for his coronation in 1804, he, like the French monarchy prior to him, sought to use the nationalistic legend of Charlemagne, whilst detaching it from royalist tradition. In order to signify the death of the Holy Roman Empire and with it German ambition, in September that year, he spent nine days in Aachen where he made a public show of respect for Charlemagne, as Otto I had done at his coronation. This moment can be viewed as the genesis of a French Empire that would seek to unite the continent under French rule.

During the previous two 'revivals' of the 'Roman Empire', under Charlemagne and Otto III, the Roman Catholic Church played a vital role: first in granting the kings the legitimacy to become emperors, and second, in enabling the essence and culture of classical Rome to fill the empire through the Roman Catholic Church. It was perhaps on the issue of legitimacy that Napoleon sent a request to Pope Pius VII to be present at the coronation. However, as with previous coronation ceremonies involving a pontiff, a divine blessing would come at a cost. Pius obliged but only after drawing up a Concordat, which was duly signed by both parties. The Concordat caused the French to surrender control of ecclesiastical appointments in return for religious freedom. The Concordat solidified the Roman Catholic Church as the majority church of France and brought back most of its civil status. In return, Pius travelled to Aachen to crown Napoleon. However, it is likely that Napoleon knew that if the pope physically placed a crown upon his head, as Pope Leo III did to Charlemagne, the debate over who should submit to whom would continue. So, during the coronation ceremony, Napoleon

Napoleon Bonaparte

reached up and took the crown from Pius and placed it on his own head! The picture was complete; the empire of the Franks and the throne of Charlemagne in Aachen had been resurrected by Napoleon after ten centuries, with the Roman Catholic Church in a marginalised position.

Napoleon, as Louis XIV had done, based much of his reign on the Roman narrative. On his coronation as emperor, Napoleon was crowned with a laurel spray like those used by the Caesars and was painted wearing it, by the aforementioned Jacques-Louis David. The idea behind such artwork was to present Napoleon as the new neo-Roman Caesar of France. When the time came for Napoleon to justify his move from rank of First Consul to emperor, he used the same process that Augustus used to transition Rome from republic to empire. Boris Johnson in his fascinating book *The dream of Rome* states:

> *He was working with a pre-existing historical narrative, in the sense that he, Napoleon, imitated the Roman move from republic to empire that took place under Augustus. Not only did Rome provide him with the iconography; it furnished a legitimating precedent for his transition to dictatorship. Rome provided the archetype for the conflict at the heart of all succeeding politics: between republicanism and Caeserism.*[92]

In Place Vendôme Paris, Napoleon had the Vendôme Column constructed to commemorate his successful victory over the Austrians at the battle of Austerlitz. One thousand two hundred and fifty Austrian cannons were melted down to create the structure, to replicate the great column of Trajan that the Romans built to commemorate their defeat of the Dacians, or modern day Romanians. Similarly, the *Arc de Triomphe* was based upon the arches found in Rome. Napoleon had his army march past both structures, in a similar way to that which the Caesars of the Roman Empire had done.

Not only had Napoleon based his victories and architecture on the archetype provided by Augustus, but he adopted the most evocative Roman symbol as the standard for his French Empire, the eagle. Napoleon had bronze eagles carried across Europe as he embarked on military campaigns. When he finally met defeat and failure in Moscow at the hands of the Russians, war poet Victor Hugo wrote: 'It was snowing and the snow had won. For the first time the eagle lowered its head...'[93]

The religious policy of the French Empire was different from the previous two 'revived Roman Empires' we have already examined. Jews living in France were allowed, and even encouraged by Napoleon to be emancipated into French society. For Napoleon, the states of Europe were to be united as a secular body, with freedom of religion granted to the individual. However, this meant that the French Empire lacked a clear spiritual dynamic, which the Roman Catholic Church had provided to the empires of Charlemagne and Otto III. As a result, if military conquest failed, the empire would have no other reason to continue. This is precisely what happened in 1815 at the Battle of Waterloo, which Napoleon lost, and following this, was exiled. The eagle, symbolising the reign of Napoleon, was purged from French political iconography, and, with it the Roman narrative that had found such a prominent place in the country's culture and arts.

Napoleon and his French Empire stand as another attempted 'revival' of the 'Roman Empire', but one that was more diluted in comparison with the Holy Roman Empire that preceded it. This dilution was due to the marginalised role of the Roman Catholic Church, which contained the essence and character of the Roman Empire.

A new precedent though had been set through the role of Napoleon - the emergence of a single nation seeking to re-unite the old Western Roman Empire following a historical Roman narrative. This precedent was set to become the pattern of many nations that were previously part of the first united Frankish kingdom: Austro-Hungary, Serbia, Bulgaria, Belgium, Russia and Britain. However, despite such other attempts to associate with the Rome of antiquity, of paramount interest to us is the immediate emergence of the German Empire in the wake of the French failure.

---

[92] Boris Johnson, *The Dream of Rome,* Second Edition, London: Harper Perennial, 2007, p.37.

[93] Victor Hugo, "The Retreat from Moscow, Trans., John Richmond", *Stephen Spender Trust,* <http://www.stephen-spender.org/stephen_spender.html> [accessed 22 Feb 2011].

CHAPTER 18

THE GERMAN EMPIRE

In 1815, Germany was one of thirty-nine political units left in the wake of the failed French Empire. Each unit sought to unite the others into a single nation. The main contenders for the task were Prussia and Austria. The appointment of Otto von Bismarck as Prime Minister, in 1862, by Prussian king William I proved a decisive moment in the unfolding of German history, for it was Bismarck who succeeded in uniting the empire under German control.

First, Bismarck defeated the Austrians in July 1866 after seven weeks of hostilities between the two states. The Austrians and their Habsburg dynasty accepted the peace terms laid out by Bismarck and formally withdrew from German affairs, and the German Confederation was dissolved. As a result the Hohenzollern dynasty of Prussia became the central power over German affairs, and pursued a policy of military armament ready for war against the French.

In 1870 Bismarck went to war against France and succeeded in leading the Germanic states to victory over their neighbours in Main and Metz in 1871. Paris surrendered and Napoleon III was exiled to England. In the conflict that had been running for centuries between the two halves of Charlemagne's empire, this defeat of the French hailed the success of the east over the west. However the success of Germany over the French was not as significant as Bismarck's ability, immediately after the French surrender, to induce German Princes to crown William I as the king of the German Empire. Now Germany was united as an empire with a figurehead, just as the French had been under Napoleon.

The icon selected to symbolise the unity of the German Empire and the defeat of the French was a twenty-eight metre high statue of Arminius, the first century 'German' warrior, which was erected in the Teutoburg Forest. Arminius, once loyal to the Caesar, united three Germanic tribes and defeated three Roman Legions and their auxiliaries, led by Publius Quinctilius Varus. It was arguably the shrewd military coup under the leadership of Arminius in the Battle of Teutoburg Forest in the first century that saw a halt to the expansion of the Roman Empire in the West, and ultimately preserved the Germanic tribes from Roman rule.

This powerful symbol serves to show how Germany managed to hold two contradictory dreams of Rome. On the one hand, Arminius represented German nationalism, which enabled them to survive the dominance of Rome, whilst on the other hand, Arminius represented the rise of the German nation as the future inheritor and heir of the Roman Empire.

Hermannsdenkmal Monument

Despite being lost from history, Arminius was rediscovered by Martin Luther, who rechristened him 'Hermann', a symbol of those who were able to resist Rome and stand victorious. Hermann again reappears in Germany after the triumph of Napoleon against the Austrians at Wargram in 1809. Heinrich von Kleist's published but unperformed play *Die Hermannsschlacht* was seen to symbolise the anti-Napoleonic German sentiment, embodied in the figure Hermann.

Once Germany was united and its figure of Arminius stood to represent its cause, Germans in Minnesota, USA asserted their cultural heritage by adopting Arminius as the symbol for all Americans of German descent. A thirty-two foot copper statue of Arminius was delivered in 1889 to celebrate the success of the vote in Congress.

Although Arminius became a figure of German nationalism, the empire he resisted became the archetype on which the German emperors based their rule. As with the Holy Roman emperors before them, the German kings adopted the title *Kaiser*, the German translation of Caesar, used from 1871 to 1918. William I sought to base the German Empire and his rule on Augustus and his great-uncle Julius. So once again, in similar fashion to the French, the German *Kaisers* adopted the eagle as their symbol, just as the Romans did in 104 BC under Marius.

The role of the Roman Catholic Church within the German Empire was different from its role in the French Empire. Bismarck became the legendary figure that he is in European history today, not because of his ability to dominate politics, but rather his ability to balance political extremes against each other to produce the desired outcome. With the exclusion of Austria from the German confederation, the balance of religion weighed in favour of the Catholics with fifty-two percent of the population in 1855, as opposed to thirty-five percent previously. This was due to the large number of Protestants living in Austria. Once Germany was united, the strength of the Roman Catholics in the German Parliament, *Reichstag*, reflected the population they represented, and stood in opposition to some of the reforms that Bismarck wanted to introduce. The most famous clash was over the education system, which Bismarck wanted to remove from clerical control. The clash became known as 'the conflict of civilisations' and soon developed into an attack on the independence of the Roman Catholic Church. This conflict of 'civilisations' brought into being a Roman Catholic political party known as The Centre. This party united men from different classes in defence of the Roman Catholic Church. There was no parallel to this party in any other European nation, as it was prepared to be German or anti-German, liberal or anti-liberal, free trade or protectionist, pacific or bellicose. Anticipating the threat such a versatile party posed to his goals, Bismarck abandoned anti-Catholic laws and allowed the Roman Catholic Church in Germany to enjoy privileges once again in return for support in the *Reichstag*.

Just as Napoleon had failed through the Battle of Waterloo, so would the German Empire fail through the First World War. Bismarck had created a culture of fear in the new empire through his election campaign of 1887: fear of France, fear of Russia, and even fear of England. He suggested that the antidote to such fear was military conquest. The German Empire responded to this fear by creating the Triple Alliance: Germany, Austro-Hungary and Italy. France responded with the Triple Entente: France, Britain and Russia. It had become clear that the continent was heading for a war that would be a repeat of the hostilities that took place in 1870-1871. When a pro-Serbian fanatic assassinated the heir to the Habsburg throne in 1914, the Austrians, with strong German support, attacked Serbia, which in turn started the First World War.

It was only when the terms of the Treaty of Brest-Litovsk in March 1918 were publicised, that Germany realised it was the victim of its own imperialism. After the Russian revolution of 1917 and with it the fall of the Russian autocracy, German High Command returned the exiled Lenin and his Bolshevik associates to Russia to stage a coup, and thus hamper the Russians' ability to resist them in the east. After a successful coup took place in November 1917, the Bolsheviks returned the favour by asking for peace negotiations with Germany, from which came the aforementioned Treaty. The Treaty of Brest-Litovsk gave Germany swathes of lands that were not rightfully theirs, together with coalmines, factories and iron supplies. Clearly the war, which claimed over thirty-seven million casualties, was an attempt by Germany to crush France and dominate Europe by force once again.

The Triple Alliance was crushed and on 11 November 1918 the guns ceased to fire. The German Empire was so decisively defeated that there was no longer a constitutionally legitimate government in Germany. The German Empire had failed and so the 'revived Roman Empire' died.

CHAPTER 19

THE THIRD REICH

The Weimar Republic was created on 11 August 1919 as the democratic body that would repair post-war Germany. However, when the terms of the Treaty of Versailles were revealed, President Scheidemann and his cabinet resigned, seeing Germany fall into further internal chaos. Under the Treaty, Germany was to return numerous lands, have its colonies taken, and a future union of Germany and Austria was forbidden. Ultimately however, it was the 'war guilt clause' that caused the failure of the Weimar Republic. The clause firmly pointed the finger at Germany as the perpetrator of the war, and therefore made it liable for the reparations that would be needed to repair the injured countries. France was the chief instigator of the clause, campaigning to its author, American President Wilson, on the need to subject Germany to hardship for its role in the war.

Although gaining some stability after 1924, the Wall Street Crash of 1929 plunged Germany once more into political and financial disarray, due to its dependence on short-term loans from abroad. Unemployment reached crippling highs from one million three hundred thousand in September 1929, to three million the following year.

During this period of turmoil, radical factions from across the political spectrum in Germany began to arise. Although too complex to discuss in detail here, one significant factor was the propagation of the 'stab in the back' myth by extreme right-wing opponents of the Republic. The widely circulated myth stated that domestic enemies such as Jews and Socialists were responsible for German losses in the war and for the harsh terms set out in the Versailles Treaty.

Amidst the chaos and political horse-trading, Adolf Hitler emerged as leader of the largest party in the Parliament, the National Socialist German Workers' Party, NSDAP, or Nazi Party as it is known today. On 30 January 1933, Hitler became the Chancellor of Germany.

In 1942 Adolf Hitler's finance minister released a compendium of papers detailing Hitler's design for a 'New Europe'. The papers included chapters and sections on 'The Common European Currency', 'Harmonisation of European Rates of Exchange', 'The European Economic Community', 'The European Agricultural Economic Order', 'A Common Labour Policy' and 'The European Regional Principle'. Such organs of state were conceived to enable the Third Reich to fulfil Hitler's dream: leading Europe and then the world for one thousand years. Clearly, Hitler, like many before him, was seeking to create a United States of Europe. This was perhaps done in accordance with the legends of Charlemagne, for Hitler personally intervened in the then current debate in Germany over Charlemagne's German ancestry, and forbade people to traduce Charlemagne as the 'butcher of the Saxons'. Hitler perhaps wanted to present a legend of a German Charlemagne that united the continent and was proud of his German heritage.

Hitler developed Nazism, an ideology in which the Aryan race was the master race that was born to rule. This race was to conquer all others and civilize the world. In this respect, the ambition of Nazism can be compared to that of the Roman Catholic Church, which sought to spread a new civilization throughout the world by the military strength of the Holy Roman Empire. Both implied a higher culture that must be adopted by conquered lands. However, it was different inasmuch that this was about racial heritage and outward characteristics rather than the profession of faith and the practice of religion.

For Germany's advanced Aryan culture to spread throughout the world, it needed to be purged of those who did not belong to it, such as gypsy communities, homosexuals and Slavic peoples. To Adolf Hitler however, this meant the eradication of Jewish people from German society. The policy in the 1930's was characterised by a series of ad-hoc measures including the attempted boycott of Jewish businesses and shops in April 1933 and the exclusion of Jews from the civil service and certain professions. However, the Nuremburg Laws of 1935 denied Jews citizenship rights and restricted marriage between Jews and Germans. The turning point in Hitler's policy towards the Jews can be seen in 'the night of broken glass', *Kristallnacht*, in November 1938, in which many Jewish homes, two hundred and fifty synagogues and seventy-five hundred business premises were looted and burned, and many Jews were killed.

It was immediately after this event that Hitler's Final Solution was implemented: an organised programme that saw millions of Jews taken to extermination camps and killed. Unlike Napoleon, who welcomed the Jews to stay in France, Hitler was responsible for the largest massacre of the Jewish people in history. This can be used to place Hitler as a type of fulfilment of the little horn of the final 'revived Roman Empire' of Daniel chapter 7, just as Emperor Nero and Titus were viewed.

A rather interesting archaeological event was taking place during this formative stage in German history. In 1878, German archaeologists started to excavate the Pergamon altar, in a process that lasted eight years. The altar, built in the second century BC, was the pinnacle of worship in Pergamon, and the very site where Jesus Christ revealed 'Satan has his throne', during his message to John on the Island of Patmos.[94] A museum was erected in Berlin in 1901 to house the altar, but was simply not large enough to accommodate the structure and the visitors who wished to visit. In addition, archaeologists then discovered the Ishtar Gate and Processional Way in Babylon, the very gateway Nebuchadnezzar had built as a doorway to hell on earth. Therefore, throughout the First World War a larger museum was built, with the doors finally opening in 1930 for visitors to see two of the most significant buildings we have referred to in our journey thus far: the Ishtar Gate and the Pergamon Altar.

The Pergamon Altar in Berlin, Germany

Although we are left to draw our own conclusions as to the significance of this event, some important observations can be made. The Babylonian priesthood emigrated from Babylon to Pergamon after the conquest of Cyrus the Great in 539 BC. Fostering the original cult of a mother-goddess and semi-divine offspring, Pergamon was important in shaping the religious foundation of the Roman Empire. In Nazi Germany, the reconstructed buildings became cultic, symbolising the struggle between good and evil – as depicted by the scene of the Gigantomachy on the friezes around the Pergamon Altar.[95] In 1934, the Pergamon Altar provided the layout and inspiration for the construction of the massive *Zeppelinfeld* Stadium in Nuremburg. The stadium was built to accommodate the Nazi conventions. Aside from its central location in Germany, Hitler had chosen the site for two reasons. Nuremburg was the unofficial capital city of the Holy Roman Empire, being the administrative centre for the continent, and as such Hitler was connecting the Third Reich with the Roman Empire of old. Moreover, Nuremburg was a capital of anti-Semitism, with numerous Jewish pogroms taking place in the thirteenth and fourteenth centuries. It was from this seat, based on the Pergamon Altar, that Adolf Hitler revoked German citizenship to all Jews in the Nuremburg laws of 1935 – arguably the first step towards the Final Solution.

Zeppelinfeld in Nuremberg, Germany

At this stage we can already see how Hitler's Germany has fulfilled two of the three facets of what had occurred in previous 'revivals' of the 'Roman Empire': a desire to dominate and unite Europe, and persecution of the Jewish people. The first corresponds with the feet of iron mixed with clay in the statue of King Nebuchadnezzar's dream, and the second with the persecution of the saints by the little horn of the final world empire in Daniel chapter 7. Both of these formed Hitler's prerogative for foreign and domestic policy and, as we have already demonstrated, were interdependent.

However, apart from adopting a Nazi variant of the German Eagle to be used as his standard, as originally used by the German emperors before him, and the prominence given to Nuremburg, there is little other evidence to suggest that Hitler sought to follow a Roman narrative. Therefore, we must now consider the third facet in relation to Hitler and his Third Reich - the role of the Roman Catholic Church in relation to this emerging empire.

The Catholic Church in Nazi Germany presents a dichotomy; it never fully supported Hitler's regime, and yet never fully condemned it, leaving commentators to make vastly divergent conclusions. On 3 August 1941, the Roman Catholic bishop of Munster, Count August von Galen, made the bold proclamation from his pulpit in St. Lambert's, Westphalia, that lists of incurables were being drawn up throughout the diocese, who were to be taken away to be murdered as part of Hitler's euthanasia programme. Galen's condemnation of Hitler's proposed programme is significant because he made his thoughts public at arguably the most censored time in the dictatorship, and as a result, such an overtly contrary message reached the ears of most of the German people. Although several prominent National Socialist leaders urged Hitler to have Galen executed as a traitor, Dr. Goebbels, Minister of Propaganda, argued, 'the population of Munster could be regarded as lost during the war, if anything were done against the bishop, and in that fear one safely would include the whole of Westphalia.'

Hitler therefore abandoned the euthanasia operation one month after the sermon was first preached. This important example demonstrates the willingness of the Roman Catholic Church in Germany to oppose Hitler's regime.

However, the Concordat between Pope Pius XII and Adolf Hitler in 1933 has sparked much debate over the role of the Roman Catholic Church in Nazi Germany. Rabbi David Dalin viewed Pope Pius XII as a 'righteous gentile' and a Jewish Study found that he had been responsible for saving at least seven hundred thousand Jews and possibly up to eight hundred and sixty thousand from Hitler's Final Solution during the war. David Hunt, the popular Christian dispensationalist author, suggests that the purpose of the Concordat was essentially for the Vatican to receive the *Kirchensteuer*, church tax, in return for not opposing the killing of German Jews and for never excommunicating Hitler from the Catholic Church.

Whether Pope Pius XII was complicit in the murder of Jews in Nazi Germany, or an opponent of the policy, has yet to be fully assessed by examining the historical evidence. However, given its historical desire for a religio-political European unity, it is possible that the Roman Catholic Church saw some potential for the fulfilment of its mission through Hitler's regime.

Catholic theologian Michael Schmaus wrote in praise of the Nazi regime after the signing of the 1933 Concordat: 'The strong emphasis on authority in the new government is something essentially familiar to Catholics. It is the counterpart, on a natural level, to the Church's authority in the supernatural sphere. Nowhere is the value and meaning of authority so conspicuous as in our holy Catholic Church.'[96]

A note by Cardinal Michael Faulhaber, congratulating Hitler three months after he came to office, can also demonstrate this identification of the Roman Catholic Church with the National Socialist regime: 'What the old parliaments and parties have failed to achieve in sixty years your broad statesman's vision had made a reality of world history in six months. This handclasp with the papacy, the greatest moral force in the history of the world, signifies a mighty deed full of immense blessing and an increase in German prestige East and West, in sight of the entire world.'[97]

Furthermore, the Roman Catholic Church gave some support to Hitler's foreign policy. When Hitler announced his departure from the League of Nations in October 1933, the Roman Catholic Church recommended loyal Catholics to support the decision and vote in favour of the move. When Hitler violated his promises to British Prime Minister, Neville Chamberlain, by moving his troops into Austria, a crowd of almost two hundred thousand enthusiastic Catholics greeted him. Their spiritual leader, Cardinal Innitzer, proceeded not only to give Hitler the assurance of support in return for the retention of the church's liberties, but also that 'Austrian Catholics would become the truest sons of the great Reich'.

There is no evidence to suggest that Hitler saw any correlation between his Third Reich and the Catholic Church. However, it is possible that there were some at the Vatican who, in seeking to return to a position of being part of the state apparatus in order to spread their brand of Christian civilisation to the world, saw the Third Reich as an entity that they needed to embrace and journey with. The sentiments of the Roman Catholic Church on this can be seen when Pope Pius XII exhorted all Catholics in the wake of Germany's war against Tsarist Russia, to fight for a 'victory that will allow Europe to breathe freely again and will promise all nations a new future'.

In this pursuit of a relationship between the Roman Catholic Church and a nation seeking to unite what was once the Holy Roman Empire there is something familiar and yet new. Previously the Roman Catholic Church would have wrestled for power and influence with the head of the 'European empire.' If this had remained the policy of the Roman Catholic Church, the history of relationships in Europe after the Second World War would have doubtless been very different. Nonetheless one more contender for a further 'revival' of the 'Roman Empire' has already appeared since 1949 and this we will consider next.

---

[94] Revelation 2:13.
[95] In Greek mythology this was the great cosmic battle between the Olympians and the giants of Chaos.
[96] Adrian Hilton, *The Principality and Power of Europe*, Second Edition, St. Ives, Cornwall: Dorchester House Publications, 2000, p.221.
[97] *Ibid.*, p.222.

CHAPTER 20

THE EUROPEAN UNION

By 1944, Germany had virtually lost the Second World War. On 30 April 1945, Hitler and his wife Eva committed suicide and a week later Germany signed its unconditional surrender. The failure of Hitler also marked the death of the attempted 'revival' of the 'Roman Empire' anticipated by the prophet Daniel.

Not only had German nationalism failed, but so also had the continent of Europe. Over forty million had lost their lives, European economies had collapsed, factories lay in ruins and the basic infrastructure needed for recovery had been destroyed. The harsh winters of 1946 and 1947 brought parts of Europe to near starvation and death. Furthermore, Europe faced the prospect of cold war after the failure of the Yalta Conference in 1945 to curb Soviet ambition, leaving Germany divided between East and West. Only the Americans and Canadians were strong enough to provide help, which came in the shape of the Marshall Plan, administered through the European Recovery Programme. The result was the erasure of trade barriers and a common coordination of the economy on the continent, which in turn stimulated a process of political reconstruction of Western Europe.

The stage had been set for the creation of what would become the European Union as we have it today. It became clear in the eyes of Jean Monnet, the proclaimed 'Father of Europe,' that the continent's survival and success rested on Germany for two reasons. First, to prevent a repeat of the carnage and decimation that had taken place in the wars, nationalism must be curbed and replaced with supranationalism, in which Germany and other European countries would be locked together in a shared continental identity. Second, if both France and Germany were economically united in their heavy industries of coal and steel, not only would they recover and in turn stimulate the economies of fellow member states, but also the prospect of war between them in the future would become unthinkable.

On 9 May 1950, French Foreign Minister, Robert Schuman, unveiled 'The Schuman Plan', in a speech prepared for him by Monnet, which declared French intentions to initiate a new working relationship with its ancient enemy, Germany, over western coal and steel. The three Benelux countries, Belgium Netherlands Luxembourg, together with Italy and Germany, supported this proposal. In April the following year the Treaty of Paris was signed, creating the European Coal and Steel Community, ECSC.

The significance of the ECSC cannot be overestimated. For the first time since Charlemagne, France and Germany were peacefully united together in a supranational body. Both nations had surrendered aspects of their sovereignty, and in doing so, their nationalism. Such surrenders paved the way for the creation of a parliamentary assembly, court, executive and the assertion of a right to make European law. The momentum of the union became federal in nature, in which political rather than just economic integration was sought. Such federal ambitions led to the Treaty of Rome, which was signed in 1957 creating the European Economic Community, EEC. It was the EEC that became the foundation upon which the European Union would be created some years later.

Johnson, in his book, 'The Dream of Rome', hails this moment in Rome as the EU inheriting the Roman Empire: 'the successful unity of a diverse territory, a single market, single currency and a political union'. The plaque, stationed above the table where the European leaders signed a second treaty on Capitoline Hill in 2004, suggests that this had in fact taken place:

> *On the 29 October 2004 in this most sacred Capitoline Hill, which is the citadel of this bountiful city and of the entire world, in this famous and august hall named after*

> *the Horatii and the Curiattii, the high contracting parties of the nations joined in the European Union signed a treaty about the form of the constitution to be adopted, so the races of Europe might coalesce into a body of one people with one mind, one will and one government.*[98]

In fact it could be argued that the EU and its current pursuit of European control and unity over member nations is comparable to that pursued by Hitler, Napoleon and Charlemagne. The significant and welcome difference between the comparisons is that co-operation and trade have replaced war. Once the Treaty of Rome was signed, the united territories it produced were almost identical to those of Charlemagne's empire.

The similarities between Charlemagne's Europe and the EU do not simply stop at landmass and geography. Adrian Hilton in his book, *The Principality and Power of Europe*, quotes from an article in the *Sunday Telegraph* on 4 May 1997 entitled 'How Brussels plans to carve up the Kingdom', to suggest that splitting Europe into regions is similar to the Roman principle of 'divide and rule.' In this ancient system, Rome divided countries into dukedoms, principalities and kingdoms, in order to ensure that power was so diversely spread, that no civil ruler would be strong enough to challenge the emperor or the pope. In addition, the single currency of Europe, the Euro, could be compared with the single unity of currency introduced to the empire by the Romans. Conquered territories were not allowed to mint the Roman coins, leaving the emperor in charge of the fiscal institutions of the empire.

The process of 'divide and rule' can also be seen as furthered by a classical Roman method of leadership, dual citizenship. The EU promotes a European citizenship in which member countries are permitting an obligatory additional citizenship to be imposed by a foreign state. In Britain, this was the case when the blue British Passport was replaced by the red, which clearly states our additional citizenship to the EU. The EU document 'A Citizen's Europe' states: 'Now that the community is turning into a Union, a third set of rights and duties is coming into being, creating a European citizenship separate and distinct from national citizenship; not taking its place but supplementing it.'[99]

However, for this to be a true 'revival' of the 'Roman Empire,' as we have understood from our study of the fourth beast in Daniel 7, there is a clear need for a figurehead who will stand in opposition against God and His people, just as there has been in the other 'revivals' we have addressed. Hilton suggests that this lead role has not yet been filled:

> *It is yet to be decided who will play Charlemagne in the new Empire, but it is to his archetypal universal monarchy that federalist political leaders look. His Holy Roman Empire was as regulated as the European Union in every aspect of economic, political and religious life, and the European oligarchy has to ensure control in all of these spheres if its power is not to be undermined. It is for this reason that none of the institutions of the EU is democratic. They were never supposed to be.*[100]

As we examine who will take this lead, it could be anticipated from history that France, Germany and the Roman Catholic Church will struggle against each other for their own candidate to fulfil this role in the emerging empire. History, however, does not always repeat itself, so we will endeavour to present a balanced picture of the aspirations of Charlemagne's Francia and the Roman Catholic Church.

When the Americans first suggested that France's economic recovery was dependent on restarting German industry, the French not only initiated partnership discussions, but also dominated the process of setting up the ECSC in French interests. It was through this new union that the French could assert control and dominance over their rival who, in their view, never fully repaid the damage they had caused in the First World War. French President Charles de Gaulle knew that this new vehicle was his mechanism to do this, and so when it came to the discussions around the transition to the EEC, he was guilty of bullying, sulking and threatening his partners to such a degree that the EEC was framed almost entirely on French interests.

For Germany, the prospect of following a federal agenda, albeit weighing heavily in France's favour, was welcomed. Germany would make gains from this union. Whereas other nations would have to surrender sovereignty, Germany had already surrendered sovereignty as a result of the Second World War. For example, Germany could no longer arm itself, except through NATO, and in 1949 was denied nuclear capability. The need to be part of a body, which could not only arm itself, but do so with nuclear weaponry, was no doubt attractive for Germany.

It can also be argued that the second reason Germany was supportive of this agenda was due to its longstanding desire and ambition to lead a united states of Europe. With centuries of German kings ruling the Holy Roman Empire, the German Kaisers of *Bismarckian* Germany held a view regarding their relationship to Europe that was different from that of other European countries. Kaiser Wilhelm II, 1888–1918, made this clear:

> *after the elimination of the British and the Jews… the result will be a united states of Europe… The hand of God is creating a new world… a United States of Europe under German leadership.*[101]

This idea of Germany leading the continent was furthered by the propaganda of Adolf Hitler and his Thousand Year Reich, as we have previously discussed.

After the Second World War, Konrad Adenauer, the German statesmen and lifelong opponent of Hitler, continued this view: 'Germany has a divine mission to save Western Europe'.[102] Adenauer founded the Christian Democratic Party, CDP, which formed the central driving force behind European integration, believing that this was now the correct way Germany could lead the continent. Helmut Kohl, Adenauer's successor within the CDP, continued this view:

> *The future will belong to the Germans… when we build the house of Europe… In the next two years we will make the process of European integration irreversible. This is a really big battle, but it is worth the fight.*[103]

It is fascinating to discover that such deliberate attempts to manipulate the agenda and the wrestle for power within the EU have not only been the product of French and German nationalism, but also the political policy of the Roman Catholic Church. By exploring the role of the Roman Catholic Church in the evolving union in Europe, it will become clear that the Church has sought to return to its previous position of power and influence it had before the Peace of Westphalia in 1648.

Since the Second World War, successive popes have sought to help create a supranational European Union. Pope John XXIII, the successor of Pope Pius XII, insisted that Roman Catholics should be at the front of such unification efforts.[104] In 1963, Pope Paul VI declared: 'Everyone knows the tragic history of our century. If there is a means of preventing this from happening again, it is the construction of a peaceful, organic, united Europe.' Later in 1975, Pope Paul VI went on to state: 'Can it not be said that it is faith, the Christian faith, the Catholic faith that made Europe?... It is there that our mission as bishops in Europe takes on a gripping perspective. No other human force in Europe can render the service that is confided to us, promoters of the faith, to re-awaken Europe's Christian soul, where its unity is rooted.'[105]

Clearly, the papacy was viewing the creation of a united Roman Catholic continent as part of their divine mission, just as their medieval predecessors had done before them. Pope John Paul II developed the mission further when he presented the vision of a modern day Holy Roman Empire, under Roman Catholic guidance. In 1979 he declared: 'Europe, despite its present long-lasting divisions of regimes, ideologies and economic systems, cannot cease to seek its fundamental unity and must turn to Christianity. Economic and political reasons cannot do it. We must go deeper.'[106] John Paul was advancing the argument that only religious unity would unite Europe, rather than just economic and political.

If the Roman Catholic Church intentionally sought this, it would have to adopt a very different policy towards other religions than we have previously examined. This is due to the fact that the EU makes no claim of being a spiritual entity; similar to that of the French Empire led by Napoleon, all religions must be welcomed equally. The decision not to include any reference to God in the EU constitution, despite its rich and inescapable Christian heritage, is an example of how the EU seeks to be independent from religion.

It is interesting that, in the midst of this, the Second Vatican Council in 1962–1965, produced *Nostra Aetate,* a publication by Pope Paul VI on 28 October 1965, detailing the change of policy towards non-Christian religions. The outworking of the policy can be seen in the World Day of Prayer for Peace, held in the Church of Saint Francis in Assisi on 27 October 1986, by Pope John Paul II. For the first time in history, over one hundred and twenty representatives of Christian denominations and other religions gathered for prayer and fasting.

Pope John Paul II then proceeded to unite different branches of Christianity, perhaps demonstrating to the EU that Roman Catholicism was a religion that could unite the continent. In his Pastoral Provision in 1980, Pope John Paul II allowed married former Episcopal priests to become Catholic priests, and accepted former Episcopal Church parishes that wished to join the Catholic Church. In 1983, Pope John Paul II became the first pope to speak in a Lutheran Church.

It was the change of relationship to Judaism in *Nostra Aetate* that most distinctively demonstrates the change that has taken place within the Roman Catholic Church. This document states that the Jews are no longer to be held responsible for the death of Jesus Christ, and should be recognised as co-heirs with Roman Catholics of the salvation promised to Abraham. Furthermore, it announces, for the first time in Catholic history, that anti-Semitism is a sin. Acting on this document, Pope John Paul II visited the Great Synagogue in Rome on 13 April 1986, and in doing so, became the first pontiff to visit a synagogue. After establishing formal diplomatic relations with the state of Israel in 1994, thus recognising it as a nation state, Pope John Paul II hosted a Holocaust memorial concert in 1994 and proceeded to visit the Western Wall and Yad Veshem in Jerusalem six years later. The pope left a message in the wall that asked the Jewish people for forgiveness for the persecutions they had received at the hand of Christians.

Although the Roman Catholic Church is actively seeking to influence and guide the EU, it is arguably a very different entity to that which produced the Christendom of the Holy Roman Empire. It could be interpreted cynically that Vatican II was merely a repetition of all that the Roman Catholic Church did when it absorbed Roman paganism following the Church's adoption by Emperor Constantine in 313. However, the policy towards those other religions, particularly the Jews, whose suffering may have previously been increased through Roman Catholic ambivalence, has now been altered. Therefore, unless there is another shift in the policy set out in *Nostra Aetate*, the Roman Catholic Church, with its widening embrace, cannot give the European Union the legitimacy to persecute that would be required by any ultimate 'revived Roman Empire' in fulfilling the prophecy of Daniel concerning 'persecuting the saints'.

The effect papal efforts have had on shaping the agenda and securing a place within the EU have been varied. Certainly, aspects of Catholic imagery have been adopted by the EU such as the Euro flag, which is inspired by the twelve stars in the halo of Mary, appearing on the Council of Europe's stained glass window in Strasbourg Cathedral. The window was then unveiled on 11 December 1955 to coincide with the Catholic feast of the Immaculate Conception. The Flag Institute examined the evolution of the flag, and its Director William Crampton confirmed a report that Leon Marchal, the then Secretary of the Council, stated: 'It's wonderful that we have got back to the Introit on the Mass of the Assumption. It's the corona stellarum duodecim (the crown of twelve stars) of the Woman of the Apocalypse.'[107]

Clearly it can be postulated that the EU is another attempted 'revival' of the Roman Empire from antiquity, continuing many of its legacies and principles in the same geographic area that Charlemagne united at the end of the first century. France, Germany and the Roman Catholic Church have all sought to play significant roles in its evolution, each for their own ends. However it is on this issue of imagery that an interesting and sinister aspect of the EU is revealed. Although, as we have demonstrated, the EU claims no spirituality, aspects of its imagery are clearly pagan and, as such, provide a clear link all the way back to where we began our journey, Babylon.

---

[98] Johnson, *Rome,* p.31.
[99] Hilton, *Principality,* p.117.
[100] *Ibid.,* p.123.

[101] John Laughland, *The Tainted Source,* London: Little Brown & Co., 1997, p.98.
[102] Hilton, *Principality*, p.39.
[103] *Ibid.*, p.39.
[104] *Ibid.*, p.36.
[105] *Ibid.*, p.36.
[106] *Ibid.*, p.34.
[107] *Ibid.*, p.55.

CHAPTER 21

BABYLON IN EUROPE

On 14 December 1999, at a cost of €470,000,000, the Louise Weiss building, accommodating the EU Parliament, was inaugurated. The building has provoked much speculation, not only due to its enormous cost, frequent lift failures and collapsing ceilings, but largely because of its sixty metre high tower. The tower has been designed to look unfinished, and faces eastwards. The official reason for this is that the tower represents the unfinished nature of the EU, which other countries will join – making the union complete. However, the tower looks almost identical to the artwork of Pieter Brueghel the Elder in 1563 depicting the Tower of Babel. Could it be that the European Parliament is meant to symbolise the tower of rebellion and opposition to God that Nimrod first built?

The Tower of Babel, by Pieter Brueghel the Elder, created in 1563

The European Parliament building, in Strasbourg, France

An official poster released by the EU, which was soon retracted, can leave us in no doubt that the symbolism of the Tower of Babel is quite deliberate. The poster is unmistakably based on Brueghel's painting, with European peoples helping to finish the tower. The slogan reads: 'Many tongues, one voice', a clear reference to the judgement of God upon the builders of the tower recorded in Genesis 11. The tower penetrates a circle of eleven inverted pentagrams. Inverted pentagrams have numerous meanings in paganism and Satanism, but generally refer to the rejection of the Godhead in favour of Satan.

Rabbi Daniel Lapin, head of the American Alliance of Jews and Christians, has examined the parallels between Nimrod's Tower of Babel and the tower situated in the Louise Weiss building. His conclusions are quite shocking. Lapin rightly states that Nimrod was a political leader seeking to unite men in defiance of God after the great flood. The Tower of Babel was the symbol of this defiance. Also, Lapin makes an intriguing comment about the materials that Nimrod used: 'They said to each other, "Come, let's make bricks and bake them thoroughly." They used brick instead of stone, and tar for mortar', (Genesis 11:3). Both bricks and stones share the same Hebrew root, but bricks are regular and stones are irregular. Both can refer to people groups: the stones to those who have liberty and are free to be different, whilst bricks represent conformists who seek to eliminate differences to become one. The mortar that holds the bricks together can also be said to symbolise materialism, sharing the same Hebrew root as matter. Nimrod sought to unite men together in a task of such magnitude, that eventually all differences would be laid aside, and the pursuit of material gain would replace any desire for God.

Clearly the EU Parliament building is a sinister re-creation of the ancient Tower of Babel, and as such, the EU must be pursuing the outcome sought by Nimrod and the builders of the original tower: a tyranny in which dependence on God was replaced with dependence on man. Just as Babel was a city of united humanity, speaking the same language and following the same religion, so also the EU seeks to unite men together in a common tongue, a common goal and a common religion.

The imagery and symbolism of Babylon in the EU does not stop at the European Parliamentary buildings themselves. Standing outside the Winston Churchill building, situated next to the Louise Weiss building, is a statue of a woman riding a beast. This image is the favoured symbol of the EU, with numerous statues, paintings and murals found in and around the European buildings of Brussels and Strasbourg. The image has also appeared on the Euro coin, German phone cards and European posters. Although it would be logical to compare this scene with that of the female prostitute seated on a beast in Revelation 17, the official EU explanation is satisfactory enough in enabling us to see its relationship with ancient Babylon.

The scene is of the famous Greek legend of Europa and Zeus, from which the Greeks gave Europe its name. According to the legend, Europa was a beautiful young maiden who was picking flowers beside the sea with a group of friends. Zeus, literally 'God the father,' was attracted to Europa and incarnated himself as a beautiful white bull and approached the group. Europa got onto the bull's back, which immediately plunged into the depths of the sea. The bull took Europa to Crete where he raped her. Europa conceived a son named Hermes.

On earth, the Greeks believed that the myth is portrayed in the landscape of Europe and in the sky by the constellations of Taurus and Pleiades. Taurus is shaped like a bull, Zeus, and the Pleiades are the string of stars that hang from the neck of Taurus, Europa.

Europa and Zeus

Interestingly, in ancient zodiacs such as those found in Babylon, Venus represents the constellation of Europa, whilst Jupiter represents Taurus. As we have already discussed, in Babylon during the time of the Akkadians, Venus was Ishtar, the 'Queen of Heaven.' Interpretation of the zodiacs commonly cited that Jupiter and Venus, literally God the father and God the mother, conceive the planet Mercury, a Messianic offspring or son of the gods.

So despite the colourful, and somewhat debased Greek myth, the European image of Europa riding Zeus the bull is a resurgence of the ancient Babylonian cult of a mother-goddess and her son, the same cult that fastened itself to Rome during its transformation from republic to empire. It is important that we consider the origin of this cult following the death of Nimrod. In the tyranny that Nimrod created, the existence of God was not questioned; rather it was his position in heaven that was challenged. It was during this defiant act of challenge, that Nimrod set man as master of his destiny, made manifest in the Tower of Babel. It was only after his death that a cult developed from which spiritual entities such as the Sky God and the Earth Mother were introduced. Therefore, it can be argued that the EU as a post-modern entity is more closely aligned to the original religion that Nimrod founded, one in which there is no rejection of a spiritual world, but a satanic emphasis on the strength and will of mankind as masters of their own fate.

As it stands, the EU is not only another 'revival' of the 'Roman Empire,' but one which shares a relationship to ancient Rome through its reference to Babylon that no other 'revival' we have examined has done. The EU is presently the home of the Pergamon Altar, the recreated Pergamon Altar in Nuremburg, the Ishtar Gate and Processional Way, the recreated Tower of Babel and the symbol of a woman riding a beast – which is a derivative of the early Babylonian cult. It would appear that despite the thousands of years that separate the two entities, the EU is becoming a modern day Babylon, just as it was said of Rome during the time of the Early Church Fathers. And yet despite this intriguing advancement in 'revival,' the EU fails, in its current disposition, to be the final phase of the fourth kingdom anticipated by the prophet Daniel. The reasons for this will provide a basis for anticipating what may happen next in world history.

Two euro coin

CHAPTER 22

WHAT HAPPENS NEXT?

The EU has no emperor or similar counterpart, which is a vital requirement for fulfilling the anticipated character of the little horn that rises from the fourth beast in Daniel 7. As it stands, the EU has evolved into a headless empire; the territory of Charlemagne has been reunited quite precisely, the European principles that Adolf Hitler conceived are now in place, and yet there fails to be a charismatic head. Such a lack was identified as early as 1957 when Paul-Henri Spaak, a key player in the establishment of the European Common Market, was purported to have said: 'What we want is a man of sufficient stature to hold the alliances of all people and to lift us out of the economic morass into which we are sinking. Send us such a man, and be he god or devil, we will receive him.'

Whether a true quote or the spurious work of anti-EU propagandists, the desire for an outstanding leader has been the subject of countless newspaper headlines, and is perhaps now a legitimate requirement. In the light of the recent economic collapse of Greece, and the failing economies of Spain and Italy, German Chancellor Angela Merkel called for the EU to become a closer political union. This would necessitate member countries releasing fiscal control to the EU to prevent a similar economic catastrophe in the future. If this indeed happens, the EU could be viewed as a federal entity, or as some proponents would wish to suggest, a 'United States of Europe.' The leader of such would clearly have power and authority not dissimilar to that of the President of the USA. Therefore, the next stage of evolution within the structure and composition of the EU will be of vital importance for what we anticipate may happen next.

Although we have made much of the unification of the countries that only Charlemagne had previously succeeded to unite, the current territory of the EU fails to meet that which we anticipate the final phase the 'revived Roman Empire' will have within its dominion. As we discussed, the western leg of the Roman Empire failed in Europe by 476, after which time, successive 'revivals' of the Western Roman Empire took place. However, in the East, the Roman Empire endured until 1453 when it fell under the crescent moon of the Ottoman invaders. To stand as a true 'revival' of the 'Roman Empire,' the EU must attempt to bridge the gap between the West and the East, just as their Roman counterparts sought to do.

The notion of providing such a bridge was certainly the intention of those who brought the EEC to life. The final resolution of the *Seven Resolutions on Political Union* adopted by The Hague in 1948 read: 'The creation of a United Europe must be regarded as an essential step towards the creation of a United World'.[108] If the EU succeeds in bringing a political union to the continent of Europe, the creation of the EU could be viewed as a decisive transition towards a future entity that unites both the western and eastern parts of the ancient Roman Empire.

It is on this very point that the role and place of Turkey is of great interest. Being home to the capital city of the Eastern Roman Empire, Constantinople, and Pergamon, Turkey would need to be in such a federation for the EU to be truly the 'revived Roman Empire.' If indeed Turkey was to join the EU, this could be seen as the wounded head of the beast coming back to life that John recorded in Revelation 13.

Prior to 1920, the idea of Turkey aligning itself with a secular union of European countries was unthinkable. Turkey was a key state in the Ottoman Empire, and bound by Islamic Sharia Law. However, in the wake of the destruction of the Ottoman Empire during the First World War, Mustafa Kemal Atatürk, regarded his country as a backward religious state with an impoverished and illiterate population. Atatürk was an entirely new proposition for Turkey - a smoker, drinker and radical politician. He became the first President of Turkey in 1923 and began a modernisation process that not only produced a republic, but one which sought to identify with the West, which to Atatürk, was a symbol of wealth and success. Amidst reforms to the law, culture and religion, Atatürk saw membership of any European initiative for economic or political union as critical in bringing Turkey from backwardness to progression.

This is precisely what happened. After the first ten founder countries, Turkey was first in line to join the Council of Europe in 1949. After taking part in the Organisation for Economic Co-operation and Development (OECD) in 1961, Turkey then became an associate member of the EEC in 1963. Finally, on 14 April 1987, Turkey formally applied to accede to the EU.

However, despite ever increasing efforts, Turkey's accession has been the source of major controversy since its initial application. Although being approved for full membership consideration in 1999, Turkey may not discover the answer until 2015. Therefore, the decision to either accept or reject Turkey will be of paramount importance to this study.

---

[108] *Ibid.*, p.79.

CHAPTER 23

THE CONCLUSION OF THE MATTER

The vision of Nebuchadnezzar in Daniel chapter 2 and the dreams of Daniel in chapter 7, present four world empires: Neo-Babylonian, Medo-Persian, Greek and Roman. The four empires span the course of human history until the second return of Jesus, with which two events will occur. First, the final leader of the fourth empire, represented by the little horn and the fourth beast, will both receive divine judgement and destruction. Second, a kingdom will be brought to earth from heaven to replace the fourth human empire.

The discourse between Gabriel and Daniel, in Daniel 9, provides an additional biblical basis for expecting a future 'Roman Empire' that will destroy a rebuilt temple in Jerusalem and persecute the Jewish inhabitants of the city. As happened previously under the ruthless hand of Antiochus IV Epiphanes, followed by Roman Emperor Titus in 70 AD, the teaching of Jesus confirms a further future expectation of this event.

The feet of the statue consisting of iron failing to mix with clay in Daniel chapter 2, finds a level of fulfilment in European history. The unification of Europe, which the Roman Empire failed to achieve, became the ambition of war and politics within Europe from that time to the present day. We discovered that the geographical area of Francia became the area from which 'revivals' of the 'Roman Empire' have emerged. As a result, both France and Germany have been viewed as seeking to continue the 'Roman Empire' throughout their histories and even at present through the political framework of the EU. Although there are numerous gaps between each 'revival,' a case can be made for the history of Europe to be viewed as one of successive 'revivals' of the 'Roman Empire'.

During each 'revival' of the 'Roman Empire', significant variations in the character of this 'empire' have been noted. First, a case was presented to demonstrate how the Roman Empire continued in the Roman Catholic Church in a spiritual form. Second, through the Christendom brought about by the Holy Roman Empire, the 'revived Roman Empire' became a political, military and spiritual entity. France and Germany then demonstrated how the 'revived Roman Empire' could be viewed as a secular military entity, led by a single nation state. Finally, the EU has displayed how the 'revived Roman Empire' can be a political and humanist entity, led by a diverse number of nations. In addition, the EU provides us with a link back to the very beginning of our journey - Babylon.

As it stands, there is still prophecy awaiting fulfilment. The EU in its current composition fails to meet the required criteria to be regarded as the final phase of the fourth kingdom of which the Bible speaks. Such a conclusion enables us to identify two areas, in addition to the future of Turkey, that require ongoing research that will bring greater clarity to this subject.

The first area is the role and place of the city of Babylon in relation to the final phase of the fourth kingdom. The Bible predicts that Babylon will in some way be connected with this final 'Roman Empire'. The prophets Isaiah and Jeremiah take two chapters each to speak of a future destruction of Babylon.[109] Their descriptions of Babylon's fate make it clear that this event has not yet happened in history. Babylon will be destroyed to such a degree that it will be uninhabitable, with even its building materials rendered unsafe for future use. Babylon has always been populated to some degree or other, and is certainly so today. The Book of Revelation also speaks of a future destruction of Babylon in chapters 17 and 18, in connection with the judgment of the final world empire. The idea of a rebuilt city of Babylon in Iraq as capital of the final world empire has been popularised by Tim LaHaye and Jerry Jenkins, in their *Left Behind* book series. Monitoring developments in Babylon will be of critical importance.

The second area is the role and place of the Roman Catholic Church within the framework of the EU. Despite centuries of Protestant criticism, which is not without warrant, the outworking of Vatican II and *Nostra Aetate* should make it impossible for the Roman Catholic Church to act, or be considered, as a religious consort to a final Satanic world empire. Despite papal ambition to influence any religious agenda the EU may have, it is likely that Europe will not only resist such efforts, but also actively pursue a humanist tyranny that is more akin to the religion of Babylon in its earliest history. The relationship between the Roman Catholic Church and the EU should be closely observed.

However, although we may find ourselves living in the final phase of human history which will see the final kingdom, Christ's kingdom, descend from heaven, it is important that we maintain a balanced interest and focus on such matters. In the prophet Daniel we find a beautiful example of such balance.

Daniel remained in the city

Daniel knew that Babylon would be conquered by the Medo-Persians. Although the change in establishment came in the most unconventional manner, Daniel only had his previous experience of bloodshed and carnage at the fall of his own nation to prepare his heart for the change that was about to take place. Even though he had retired from service and no doubt had ample resources that would have enabled him to leave, Daniel remained in Babylon before the great transition in empires took place. Clearly the Hebrew prophet was not fearful of what would take place, nor did fine living and his honorary status compromise him. Instead, Daniel viewed his position in Babylon as God ordained and therefore he continued his ministry there.

For those of us living in Europe, and in particular in the nations of France and Germany, we must not allow the tide of world events to intimidate us into leaving in the hope of finding more peaceful lands. Rather, like Daniel, we should apply ourselves to seeking the face of God and walking with integrity before Him.

Daniel maintained a testimony

Just as the menorah lampstand was intended to burn continuously in the temple in Jerusalem to symbolise the knowledge of God, Daniel was a lamp of testimony to the ruling powers of both the Neo-Babylonian and Medo-Persian Empires. It was his willingness to exalt the Lord in the presence of Nebuchadnezzar that established Daniel in Babylon, and his courage in greeting King Cyrus with the scroll of Isaiah that secured his position in this new empire.

Quite literally, the leaders of the two successive world powers came to a place of conviction that the God Daniel served so devoutly was sovereign over all. In the case of Nebuchadnezzar, some believe that it was Daniel who mentored the king during his season of mental derangement, in which he became like a wild animal. According to this perfectly plausible conjecture, Daniel encouraged the king to turn to the Lord in order to be restored. In the course of time Nebuchadnezzar duly humbled himself and had what we might call today a conversion experience, which he detailed in a letter that was disseminated throughout the world. Although we have less detail concerning Daniel's relationship with Cyrus, we do know that he made such an impression on the Persian king that Cyrus initiated the re-building of the temple in Jerusalem.

Perhaps the greatest testimony that Daniel left in the great empires that appeared on the stage of world politics was his unwavering and unabashed devotion to God. After his initial selection to serve Nebuchadnezzar, he and his three companions risked their lives in relation to the law of God not to eat food offered to idols. Again, when it came to the issue of prayer, Daniel willingly accepted the punishment of death by lions rather than not commune with his God daily.

Yet in all this, Daniel was never bellicose in his actions, nor was he subversive. In this regard he can be likened to Christ at his crucifixion, asking the Father not to hold the actions of his persecutors, which they had committed in ignorance, against them. Daniel knew from his angelic revelations that his battle was not against flesh and blood, but against angelic forces warring in heavenly places. Furthermore, he also knew that his God was in control.

It is important that we consider how we might bear testimony to our rulers and leaders, regardless of the political agenda they seek to pursue. Should the time come when we cannot comply with a law of the land due to our submission to a higher law, we must do so with the integrity and grace that Daniel had. It was no doubt his integrity and devotion to God that prompted the respect and friendship of the pagan kings Daniel served. The Church should therefore regard such times of opposition as opportunities to reveal outwardly the beautiful work of grace that Christ has worked within; to make manifest the manifold wisdom of our God to rulers and authorities in heavenly places, (Ephesians 3:10).

Daniel revealed a future hope

Daniel knew that times of unprecedented hardship faced his descendants, namely those who would live during the days of the little horn of chapter 8, whom we have identified in history as Antiochus IV Epiphanes. Despite this morbid knowledge, Daniel discovered the most glorious hope; a hope so great it gave courage to the Jewish nation facing the relentless storm of hostility during the Maccabean era.

During his discourse with the angel Gabriel about the seventy weeks, Daniel was taught that the Anointed One, the Messiah, would come and die on behalf of the Jewish nation. As we discovered in our survey of the Gospels, the Anointed One was, and is, Jesus Christ. Jesus was also the one 'like a son of man' Daniel had seen in heaven, handing an eternal kingdom to his people. The mystery had now been unveiled; Daniel knew the mission of the Messiah. The Messiah had to come from heaven as a man during the fourth kingdom. Then, the Anointed One must die on behalf of his people. Following his death, the Messiah would one day return to earth, whilst the fourth kingdom is in its final stage, and bestow upon his people the eternal kingdom which would mark the end of the age.

It was this most glorious message of hope that Daniel embedded into the Magi, the religious priesthood of the Medo-Persian Empire. This body formed the central administration of the vast Persian Empire. Daniel's title under Darius the Mede was *Rab-mag*, Chief of the Magi.

It was during this career that Daniel founded a secret sect of the Magi and entrusted to them the revelation of the coming Messiah.

The revelation of the Messiah Daniel received unlocked Old Testament prophecy concerning world redemption. Micah spoke of Bethlehem being the town from which would come 'one who will be ruler over Israel, whose origins are from old, from ancient times', (Micah 5:2). The Book of Numbers records Balaam's oracles, in which he spoke concerning the sign of the Messiah: 'A star will come out of Jacob, a sceptre will rise out of Israel', (Numbers 24:17). By using his revelation, Daniel instructed his sect about the precise time and location the Anointed One would enter the world. Some five hundred years after Daniel's death, Magi arrived from the east and appeared before King Herod asking: 'Where is the one who has been born king of the Jews? We saw his star in the east and have come to worship him', (Matthew 2:2).

Daniel did not preoccupy himself and his priestly sect with fear of future events. Rather he looked with gladness and anticipation upon the glory that God would reveal through His Messiah who would come to save the world. As we consider the storms that we may face, like Daniel, we should joyfully speak of the return of our great king. Although diligent time should be spent searching the Holy Scriptures to learn more about his coming, we should equally spend our strength in sharing his gospel to prepare mankind for his return. When we fully give ourselves to this end, the stone shall finally strike the feet of the image and the most glorious new age will begin: 'And this gospel of the kingdom will be preached in the whole world as a testimony to all nations, and then the end will come', (Matthew 24:14).

---

[109] Isaiah 13-14; Jeremiah 50-51.

SELECT BIBLIOGRAPHY

Anderson, Robert, *Daniel, Signs and Wonders*, Grand Rapids, Michigan: Wm. B. Eerdmans Publishing. Co., 1984.

Baldwin, Joyce G., *Daniel, An introduction and commentary*, Westmont, Illinois: InterVarsity Press, 1978.

Becher, Matthias, *Charlemagne,* Translated by David S. Bachrach, Yale, Great Britain: Yale University Press, 2003.

Blair, Alasdair, *The European Union since 1945*, London: Pearson Longman, 2005.

Boutflower, Charles, *In and around the Book of Daniel*, New York and Toronto: The Macmillan Co., 1923.

Braverman, Jay, *Jerome's Commentary On Daniel, A study of comparative Jewish and Christian Interpretations of the Hebrew Bible*, The Catholic Biblical Quarterly Monograph Series 7, Washington, America: The Catholic Biblical Association of America, 1978.

Bryce, James, *The Holy Roman Empire*, Cambridge, Massachusetts: Macmillan and Co., 1887.

Cachemaille, E. P., *The First Two Visions of Daniel*, London: Charles. J. Thynne, 1928.

Cachemaille, E. P., *XXVI Present Day Papers on Prophecy; An explanation of the visions of Daniel and of the Revelation, on the continuous – historic system*. London: Seeley, Service & Co., LTD., 1911.

Collins, Roger, *Charlemagne*, London: Macmillan and Co., 1998.

Dalman, G., *The Words of Jesus,* English Translation by Kay, D. M., Edinburgh: T. & T. Clark, 1909.

Davies, Glyn, *A History of Money from Ancient Times to the Present Day*, Cardiff: University of Wales Press, 1996.

Detweiler, Donald S. *Germany: A Short History,* Third Edition, Revised, Illinois: Southern Illinois University Press, 1999.

Dinan, Desmond, *Origins and Evolution of the European Union*, Oxford: Oxford University Press, 2006.

Dodd, C. H., *According to the Scriptures*, First Edition, London: Nisbet & Co., LTD., 1952.

Driver, S. R., *The Book of Daniel with Introduction and Notes*, Cambridge, Massachusetts: Harvard University Press, 1920.

Dyer, Charles H., *The Rise of Babylon,* Cambridge: Tyndale House Publishers, 1991.

Elon, Amos, *The Pity Of It All, A Portrait of German Jews 1743-1933*, St. Ives, Cornwall: Penguin Books, 2002.

Foxe, John, *The New Foxe's Book of Martyrs,* rewritten and updated by Harold J. Chadwick, Alachua, Florida: Bridge-Logos Publishers, 1997.

Fulbrook, Mary, *A Concise History of Germany*, Second Edition, Cambridge: Cambridge University Press, 2004.

Fyall, Robert, *Daniel*, Tain, Scotland: Christian Focus Publications, 1998.

Gibbon, E. *Decline and Fall of the Roman Empire*, Book VI, New York: Penguin USA., 1983.

Gillingham, John, *European Integration 1950–2003. Superstate or New Market Economy?* Cambridge: Cambridge University Press, 2003.

Goldingay, John, E., *Daniel, Biblical Commentary*, Volume 30, Dallas, Texas: Word Books, 1989.

Gurney, Robert, *God in Control*, Worthing, West Sussex: H. E. Walter LTD., 1980.

Hathaway, David, *Babylon in Europe*, Bognor Regis, West Sussex: New Wine ministries, 2006.

Heather, Peter, *The Fall of the Roman Empire. A New History*, First Edition, Oxford: Oxford University Press, 2006.

Heaton, E. W., *The Book of Daniel; Introduction and Commentary*, London: SCM Press LTD., 1956.

Hendriksen, William, *More than Conquerors*, Commemorative Edition, Grand Rapids, Michigan: Baker Book House, 1982.

Henry, M., *Commentary on the whole Bible,* Complete and Unabridged, Peabody, Massachusetts: Hendrickson Publishers, Inc, 1991.

Hilton, Adrian, *The Principality and Power of Europe. Second Edition.* St. Ives, Cornwall: Dorchester House Publications, 2000.

Hislop, Alexander, *The Two Babylon's or The Papal worship proved to be the worship of Nimrod and his wife,* Popular Edition, Topeka, Kansas: S.W Partridge & CO., 1952.

Hunt, Dave, *A Woman Rides the Beast*, Eugene, Origen: Harvest House Publishers, 1994.

Johnson, Boris, *The Dream of Rome,* Second Edition, London: Harper Perennial, 2007.

Johnson, Paul, *A History of the Jews*, New York: HarperCollins Publishers, 1987.

King, Geoffrey R., *Daniel, A detailed explanation of the book*, Worthing, West Sussex: Henry, E. Walter Ltd., 1966.

Lacocque, Andre, *The Book of Daniel*, London: SPCK, 1979.

LaHaye, Tim & Jenkins, Jerry B., *Left Behind, Book One,* Carol Stream, Illinois: Tyndale House Publishers, Inc., 1995.

Lang, G.H, *The Histories and Prophecies of Daniel*, Fourth Edition, London: The Paternoster Press, 1950.

Laughland, J., *The Tainted Source*, London: Little Brown & Co., 1997.

Leupold, H. C., *Exposition of Daniel*, Thirteenth Printing, Grand Rapids, Michigan: Baker House Company, 1969.

Michael, Robert, *Holy Hatred: Christianity, Anti-Semitism, and the Holocaust*, New York: Palgrave Macmillan, 2006.

Miller, P., *The Divine Warrior in Early Israel*, Cambridge, Massachusetts: Macmillan and Co., 1973.

Monwinckel, Sigmund, *He that Cometh*, Grand Rapids, Michigan: Wm. B. Eerdmans Publishing. Co., 1954.

Parker, Philip, *The Empire Stops Here*, London: Jonathan Cape, 2009.

Philip, James, *By the Rivers of Babylon Parts I & II*. Aberdeen, Scotland: Didasko Press, 1972.

Porteous, Norman, *Daniel*, Second Edition, London: SCM Press ltd., 1979.

Pusey, Edward, *Daniel the Prophet*, New York: Funk & Wagnalls, 1891.

Ratzinger, Joseph, *Europe Today and Tomorrow, Addressing the Fundamental Issues*, Second Edition, San Francisco: Ignatius Press, 2005.

Roth, Michael, *Facing the Patriarch in Early Davidian Painting. Rediscovering history: culture, politics, and the psyche*, Palo Alto, California: Stanford University Press, 1994.

Rowley H. H., *Darius the Mede and the Four World Empires in the Book of Daniel, A historical study of contemporary Theories*, Eugene, Oregon: Wipf & Stock Publishers, 2006.

Rupp, Gordon, *Martin Luther and the Jews,* A Pamphlet, London Council of Christians and Jews, 1972.

Skevington, Wood, A., *Signs of the Times; Biblical Prophecy and Current Events,* Second Impression, Lakeland, Florida: Lakeland Publishers, 1971.

Tanner, Joseph, *The Chart of Prophecy and our place in it*, London: Hodder and Stoughton, 1898.

Taylor, A.J.P., *The Course of German History*, Cornwall: Routledge Publishers, 2001.

Unger, Merrill, F., *Unger's Bible Handbook*, First Edition, Chicago: Moody Press, 1966.

Wessels, Anton, *Europe: Was it Ever Really Christian?* London: SCM Press Ltd., 1994.

Whitcomb, John, C., Jr., *Darius the Mede.* International Library of Philosophy and Theology. Biblical and Theological Studies Series. Philadelphia, Pennsylvania: P & R Publishing Company, 1963.

Wilcock, Michael, *I saw heaven opened, The message of Revelation*, First Edition, Westmont, Illinois: Intervarsity Press, 1975.

Wilson, Derek, *Charlemagne, Barbarian and Emperor*, Surrey: Pimlico, 2006.

Wilson R. D., *Studies in the Book of Daniel*, New York and London: G. P Putnam's sons, 1917.

Wright, C. H. H., *Daniel and His Prophecies*, London: Williams & Norgate, 1906.

The Wycliffe Bible Commentary, First Edition, London: Oliphants, 1969.

Young, E. J., *Daniel's vision of the Son of Man*, London: The Tyndale Press, 1958.

Young, E. J., *The Prophecy of Daniel*, Grand Rapids, Michigan: Wm. B. Eerdmans Publishing. Co., 1949.